D0945836

Parenting the AD/HD Child:
A New Approach

Parenting the AD/HD Child:

A New Approach

By
Eduardo M. Bustamante, Ph.D.

PARENTING THE AD/HD CHILD: A NEW APPROACH. Copyright © 1997 by Eduardo Bustamante. All rights reserved. Printed in the United States of America. No part of this book may be used or reproduced in any manner whatsoever without written permission except in case of brief quotations embodied in critical articles or reviews. For information, address Whitcomb Publishing, 32 Hampden Street, Springfield, MA 01103

Cover design by Vito Gramarossa

ISBN: 0-9633007-4-1

LIbrary of Congress Catalogue No: 97-62018

Dedication

I dedicate this book to the many beautiful people trapped unnecessarily in a destructive and demoralizing family situation due to problems involving children who are having difficulty growing up. I wish you mothers, fathers, and youths the empowerment to live a fuller life, and offer you a simple piece of the puzzle — a new perspective on parenting and family living.

Contents

Acknowledgments

I am very grateful to Carroll Robbins for giving this manuscript the polish it needed. His careful editing by far exceeded my expectations. I am in awe of his ability to revise and correct. He was able to accomplish in a few weeks what I had spent years pursuing. His work by far exceeded my vision of what this book could be.

As thankful as I am to Carroll Robbins for his editing, I am even more grateful to him for having brought his daughter, Chris Hamilton, into this world. Chris became my champion. I will always remember when she first pledged to make my work known. Like many parents before her, she felt I was on to something, and wanted to help. Unlike the others, however, she made it happen. She introduced me to her brother, Paul Robbins, president of Whitcomb Publishing Co., and that fortunate encounter led to the publication of this book.

I never would have come to know Chris Hamilton, however, if it weren't for another unique individual, Sandi Kupperman. Sandi studied my work years ago, and founded the Family Support Center, in Longmeadow, Massachusetts, to help disseminate it. She has supported my work in countless ways for years. She has been on a path to enlightenment that has rubbed off on me. She will always be a source of inspiration to me. Sandi helped Chris handle problems with her troubled son, and sponsored me to conduct workshops. This is where I met Chris.

There would not have been a center in which to develop my work if it weren't for Mark Bulkin. Mark made it his personal business to advance my work. He traveled with me for almost two years, taping my talks and workshops, and coaching me on how to clarify my delivery. He pulled my clinic in Amherst, Massachusetts, out of the organizational and financial rut into which it had fallen. He invested the money and effort necessary to make the business efficient. His support freed me to pursue my work without distractions.

My brother, Andrew, has been another key player in the development of this program. He trained under me for some three years, and became one of the first individuals to implement the program successfully. He managed the Amherst center for two years, and has directed our research efforts ever since.

Ted and Robin Diamond were also sources of inspiration in the writing of this book. Ted helped me write important parts of the book, and offered me excellent advice and support along the way. He gave my work a tremendous boost, at a time when it sorely needed it. He came up with the concept of *Natural-Consequences Parenting*, and offered me priceless support and encouragement.

Barton Herzkowitz, M.D., has also made important contributions to the development of this program. He helped validate the work by becoming one of the first clinicians to successfully replicate it. He sponsored workshops in the Boston area, and helped make the work known there. He made suggestions on how to pull this material together into a coherent book, and has collaborated with our research efforts.

Contributors like Dr. Herzkowitz, and Sandi Kupperman would not have been possible without Kathryn Dunn, Joan Linden, Shari O'Brien, and Michael Flynn, all of whom were instrumental in the founding of the Family Team Development Center in Amherst, the first facility established to research and develop this program.   Kathy, Joan, and Michael helped edit earlier versions of this book.

Kevin Osborne helped write the segments in this book on *Make-Sure Parenting*, and the *Natural-Consequences Parenting* attitude. Although we never had the opportunity to co-author a book, his writing was a true gift.

None of this would have been possible if it weren't for Robert Mendelsohn, Ph.D. Dr. Mendelsohn is dean of the Derner Institute at Adelphi University, where I received my doctorate. He was my teacher, supervisor, and mentor in brief therapy. He taught me everything I needed to put this program together. I must also give credit to another key mentor, Robert Schenk. Bob trained me in adolescent treatment. He introduced me to the notion that children would turn out best without all the neurotic control that most of us exert over our kids. He also introduced me to the idea of natural development, which I initially resisted, but eventually grew to appreciate.

I would be remiss if I didn't also acknowledge the contribution of the many kids I have treated over the years. They have taught me a great deal, and continue to do so. They let me know when I am on target, and when I am off the mark. Their trust in me strengthened my resolve and gave meaning to my work. They are my basic source of inspiration.

My final acknowledgment is to my wife, Hilda, and our three children, Eddie, Ande and Laura. Their patience and honest feedback have proven invaluable. They have been patient with me during the far too many hours I have worked. They did without so that I could put much of our family resources into the research and development of this program. There are many other parents and children who have made important contributions to my work.

To all of them, I give special thanks.

Introduction:
A Message to Parents

The purpose of this book is to share with you a new approach to parenting that will allow you to enjoy your children as never before. The methods described will promote confidence among the members of your entire family, and help you attain one of parenting's greatest rewards — watching your children realize their full potential. The book focuses on Attention Deficit/Hyperactivity Disorder (AD/HD), and tells how to cope with this problem and reshape the lives of children who suffer from it. It doesn't matter, however, whether your children are easy to live with, shy, difficult, oppositional, or AD/HD. The insights presented in this book will help you bring out the best in them.

The kind of parenting proposed comes from my work over a fifteen-year period with AD/HD-afflicted and other challenging children. The problems I encountered dealing with them and their families compelled me to experiment with methods I otherwise never would have considered. I studied neurophysiology and the process of rehabilitation. I worked to understand how brain functions develop, and how children mature. Eventually I got a glimpse of a unique process — the splendor of natural development.

I have dedicated the last five years of my life to discovering how abilities unfold in children when they are allowed to develop naturally, in their own time, with the least possible help from adults. I have developed the assumptions that abilities, and the motivation to exercise them, launch themselves — in their own time; that we have achieved very little by forcing children to fulfill obligations before the drive to do so has come from within themselves; and that persistent rushing and pressuring does very little to accelerate development, and can actually retard the process if the pressure is great enough.

My initial observations proved so encouraging that I felt empowered to test these assumptions further. Moving cautiously, I sought to determine the level of parental control needed to raise healthy children. I couldn't begin, however, by attempting the extreme — just allowing children to roam free and unsupervised. That much was clear. But how much control was really necessary? That was a most challenging question.

I have been particularly inspired by observing the natural process take place in my own son, who has AD/HD, and of whom I have every reason to be proud. My son has not taken Ritalin, a widely used medication which has a temporary normalizing effect on the brain in AD/HD children. Nor has he had any special educational services, ever! He had good and forgiving elementary school experiences. However, since middle school he has experienced failure in numerous ways. As a result, he has felt the need to develop AD/HD-related brain functions, and he has succeeded. My friends who have younger children express admiration for the person my son has become. They say they would love to see their non-AD/HD children turn out like my boy. Others who know my family compliment my wife and me on all three of our children.

My daily observations have remained a source of inspiration for me, despite the many years of witnessing the same phenomenon. I continue to be amazed by the splendor of each ability I see unfolding naturally in my children. I have seen the same splen-

dor in the kids I treat in my practice. Children allowed to develop
their abilities naturally remain content and confident. They can exercise these abilities vigorously for hours, with minimal distress. They
accept related obligations in ways that surprise me and make everyone proud. They love to communicate about their accomplishments.

The parenting program presented in this book is designed to
help you realize the benefits of natural development with your
own children. It is based on sound psychology. Each of its components is based on a scientific discovery that advanced the thinking of its day, and has since remained the standard of the experts.
The advances surveyed in this book have given rise to the most
important theories in child psychology, including: Attachment,
Self-Esteem, Family Satisfaction, Behavior Modification, and Cognitive Learning Theories. Each chapter introduces a critical advance in child-rearing literature. Each tells the story behind one
of these discoveries, and describes the impact it had on its time.
Each derives useful applications from the breakthrough presented.
The depth of knowledge you will derive from these discoveries
will allow you to truly understand what you're doing. This will give
you the confidence you will need to continue with the program.

The first breakthrough reviewed in *Parenting the AD/HD Child:
A New Approach* establishes the singular importance of developing adaptive brain functions in children. This book refers to activity in the adaptive brain as *make-sure* functions.

Parenting the AD/HD Child pinpoints the besetting problem of
Make-Sure Parenting, common among families with challenging
children. *Make-Sure Parenting* is one of the main reasons why
parenting programs have often failed, especially with AD/HD,
and other difficult children, including teenagers. Make-sure functions are so important, and adults possess such a great ability to
execute them, however, that society expects parents to perform

them for their children.

Indeed, as a result of societal pressures many parents end up micromanaging their children's lives. They shepherd their children through daily routines with seemingly successful results. But, despite appearances, they are committing the grave error of inhibiting the development of their child's own critical *make-sure* functions. They interfere with the maturation process, induce oppositional behavior in even normal children, and encourage rebellion. *Make-Sure Parenting* will probably not create a lasting problem for easy-to-rear children, but it will for those with AD/HD.

Parenting the AD/HD Child introduces *Natural-Consequences Parenting* as the remedy for the problems of *Make-Sure Parenting*. *Natural-Consequences Parenting* will help children develop strong *make-sure* functions of their own, and relies on the tenets of Attachment Theory for its effectiveness. The book also introduces a method of parental behavior called the *Natural-Consequences Attitude*, which can best be described as playful, but not helpful. The playfulness buffers the child's emotional and attachment system against trauma. At the same time, the non-helpfulness challenges the child to exercise vital *make-sure* functions for himself by employing his frontal, or adaptive, brain. The book clarifies the importance in this process of inducing the right kind of anxiety in the child to encourage the exercise of vital *make-sure* functions, and facilitate brain maturation.

Parenting the AD/HD Child will show you how to surround your children with consequences that teach and strengthen. The book turns to a combination of Behavior Modification and Cognitive Learning Theories to achieve this end. You will learn to apply the same effective psychology behind Time Out to children of different ages, and special situations, when it becomes necessary to separate them from regular activities. This section shares much in common with leading behavioral programs, except that the emphasis is on strengthening rather than on subsidizing. Established programs developed in the past share the conviction that exposing your children to natural and reasonable consequences stemming from their behavior is a critical component of effective parenting. To that, however, I add a cognitive element to facilitate the development of important abilities, namely, to learn from experience, feel concern, and develop a conscience.

Parenting the AD/HD Child shows you how to expose unruly children to reasonable consequences without hurting them. The chapter on consequences emphasizes the value of putting children in charge of themselves, and teaching them how to see failures as learning opportunities.

Parenting the AD/HD Child combines all of the above developments into a working model for everyday use. The program tells how to prepare consequences. It shows you how to put your children in charge, how to escape conflict-laden situations, and how to decide whether to allow consequences to take place, or to dispense them. A trouble-shooting section will help you resolve the two most common obstacles to successful implementation of this program: excessive oppositional defiance, and a condition I call parental neurosis. Finally, it shows you how to use your family unit to encourage social skills.

The older established methods have demonstrated their effectiveness with the common parenting difficulties of "normal" children. However, they have failed with AD/HD, other difficult children, and adolescents. You will find that easier to rear children respond eagerly to this program, and grow from it in ways that will surprise you. You will be more than surprised when you see that the program works equally well with AD/HD and other difficult children. Enjoy the book and enjoy your children.

1   The All-Important *Make-Sure* Brain Functions

Make no mistake about it, there is one objective in child rearing that towers above the rest — the development of strong *make-sure* brain functions. These functions literally define maturity. The recently published work on emotional intelligence serves as a testament to their importance. These mental functions provide the foundation for emotional intelligence, and emotional intelligence is the foundation of success in life. Once children develop these abilities, they are free to apply them to any skill they wish.

The ability to make sure something is done properly involves adaptive brain functions — those that help us adapt to challenging conditions. To *make sure* something happens, one must deploy these *make-sure* functions. Think about what you have to do to make sure something takes place properly. You must inhibit desires and emotions, curb arousal, plan your course of action, find motivation, initiate effort, sustain attention, sustain effort, organize, attend to details, anticipate problems, solve problems, choose an adaptive course of action, communicate with others, and double-check all aspects of the project at hand until success is certain.

Parents are asked repeatedly to perform these *make-sure* functions for their children. Schools and other institutions, and members of other families constantly tell you to make sure your children do this, that, and the other thing. As a result, it often takes a couple of decades for children to develop mature, adult-like, *make-sure* abilities. Developing these abilities is clearly more important than learning reading, math, violin, or a foreign language, although these forms of learning are not mutually exclusive. All too often, however, parents confuse priorities. They put other forms of learning ahead of ensuring the ultimate development of *make-sure* functions. In this book, you will come to realize what a mistake this can be.

The difference between established approaches to child rearing and the approach presented in this book is simple: Established approaches use behavioral technologies to supplement weak brain functions in children. The method described in *Parenting the AD/HD Child* employs similar tactics, but employs them to strengthen weak brain functions. This difference becomes most important in dealings with AD/HD children.

Leading theorists have established AD/HD as a disability, and suggested "prosthetic devices" in the form of structures, reminders, rewards and punishments to supplement deficient brain functions, and to help these children function effectively in traditional family and classroom settings. Their primary focus remains on short-term goals. That is, get the children through the day. This strategy offers opportunities to keep these children sufficiently educated and informed, but in the long run tends to become a struggle. It also robs them of their opportunity to exercise the brain functions that are most impaired. Thus, they remain weak in their own must-do abilities.

My observations suggest that supplementing brain functions for AD/HD children not only causes these functions to remain weak, but also fosters excessive dependency, and often causes deviant behavior and emotional problems. These children learn to exploit their supporters, and, over time, come to feel increasingly defiant. This facilitates a progression from AD/HD to Oppositional-Defiant Disorder (ODD), and to Conduct Disorder, a clinical name for delinquency.

The problems of atrophying brain functions and emotional problems can account for the poor outcome of treatment efforts with AD/HD children as reported in the literature. Studies based on these approaches show they have uniformly yielded poor results in the long run. The approaches work in clinics, but fail to reflect life outside the treatment room, probably because the subject youths are not developing their native abilities. These methods are rated as tedious to implement. On the whole, treatments for AD/HD and ODD "have shown little demonstrated utility" (to quote Abikoff, a leading researcher in AD/HD). The long-term prognosis for these children is alarmingly poor, and the potential for unpleasant societal consequences is great.

For years, I have been testing the hypothesis that AD/HD children will strengthen weak brain functions, given the right conditions. I am now confident that this is so. However, these children will not exercise vital brain functions unless the conditions are right for them to do so. I have spent years testing a variety of ways to encourage AD/HD children to do things for themselves. I have seen these children respond to some of these methods with enthusiasm. They have grown in confidence, strength, wisdom and self-esteem. However, the process has taken time.

The formula for strengthening *make-sure* functions involves three components: (1) allowing the children to choose activities that will provide opportunities for them to exercise strengths, and in which they can take pride; (2) putting them in charge of performing their own *make-sure* functions; and (3) using smart consequences with a noncontrolling, accepting attitude to promote social skills.

Intervention methods tried previously with AD/HD children have proven tedious to implement, and have consistently delivered long-term failures, despite some short-term benefits. The program aimed at developing *make-sure* functions, on the other hand, has proven easy to implement. It has produced short-term failures, but long-term successes. Short-term failures resulted from putting children in charge of themselves at a time when they still lacked the maturity and strength needed to succeed on their own. Long-term successes have come through the sustained effort children make in the strengthening and maturing process, once they are in charge and have turned responsibilities into challenges.

The next chapter will open your eyes to the stunning repercussions of subjecting your AD/HD or oppositional-defiant child to a parenting approach I refer to as *Make-Sure Parenting*. *Make-Sure Parenting* occurs when parents follow the advice of experts who recommend that they supplement weak brain functions. *Make-Sure Parenting* will hinder the development of children, and leave them prone to oppositional disorders.

2 The Hidden Cause of Most Child-Rearing Problems

Society assumes that parents have an obligation to perform *make-sure* functions for their children. *Make-sure* functions are extremely important, and parents obviously are much more capable of performing them than their children. The children, it is assumed, will learn through the example of the parents how to perform these functions for themselves. This assumption, however, leads to a parenting method that is fundamentally flawed. It may work well with easy children who live for opportunities to please their parents. Parents who use this approach with challenging children, however, don't stand a chance. This chapter will explain why.

The Two Commandments of Parenting

Most parents understandably regard the well-being of their children as of paramount importance. They dedicate themselves to this cause with an almost religious fervor, and reverently adhere to what can be referred to as the two commandments of parenting.

The first commandment is, "Thou shalt protect thy child," the second, "Thou shalt educate thy child." The instinct to protect their children is so deeply ingrained and such a passionate concern for parents that the second commandment serves primarily to further the protective function of the first. Parents teach their children incessantly, hoping to spare them the harsh consequences of ignorance as they become adults.

Unfortunately, parents' teachings, their logical, well-constructed arguments, and their lectures all too often fall on deaf ears. This is because adults and children live in two distinct worlds, and speak two different languages. Parents engage in folly when they attempt to speak the language of logic to children, who only desire immediate gratification. For, in pursuit of their own gratification, children, and especially those with AD/HD, will systematically override all adult arguments and grown-up logic, hoping that this will cause their parents to give up their efforts to instruct and control.

The Philosophy of Make-Sure Parenting

The two commandments of parenting have given rise to a child-rearing philosophy I call *Make-Sure Parenting*. As the name suggests, parents who subscribe to this philosophy strive to make sure their children do everything correctly. Their philosophy is rooted in the misguided belief that children can be molded into being good.

The term *Wheel of Life* serves as a metaphor for how parents in our society are always on the go. Get up in the morning; make sure the kids are up on time; make sure they have their clothes ready, the right clothes; make sure they eat breakfast, a healthy breakfast. Once the kids are on the bus, the parents have to go on about their own affairs, probably put in a hard day's work, and, in addition to everything else, make sure that after-school child-care is in place.

After school, the parent must make sure the kids do their homework. There are always notices from school about all kinds of activities — Scouts, basketball, soccer, swimming, religious. All of these entail transportation, practices, registrations, games and parents' meetings. Parents must make sure all activities are well coordinated and successful. The kids must have snacks, dinner must be prepared. Of course, there is laundry, too, and the house must be picked up. Kids must be bathed. They must all eat a good meal — another *make sure*. Clear the table, do the dishes, clean up the kitchen. Make sure the children get to bed on time. They all need a bedtime story. Teeth must be brushed, pajamas located and donned, backs scratched, and fears of the dark allayed. Once the children are asleep, the parent can finally open that letter from the IRS, maybe exercise, maybe even talk to a friend by phone.

In directing all this activity, the parent is exercising a series of vital brain functions that are weak in AD/HD children, including the ability to inhibit impulses and emotions, plan, prepare alternate plans to compensate for error, organize, sustain attention, sustain effort, monitor progress, anticipate problems, solve problems, make moral judgments, attend to details, and double-check to make sure everything went well. These mental abilities virtually define maturity, or emotional intelligence, and fostering their development in the child is the single most important objective in parenting.

Most parents want to see their children function in a mature way. Yet, by performing *make-sure* functions, many interfere with the development of the children's ability to satisfy their needs independently. They prevent AD/HD children from having to exercise and strengthen these functions. The end result can be children who achieve success in areas including academics, sports and social relationships, but lack drive, and remain weak in their ability to manage other essential aspects of their own lives. Such children will lose confidence as soon as they must face responsibility without Mom being around. Their self-doubts stem from never having accomplished things on their own.

When stakes are high, it will be hard for *Make-Sure Parents* to place their faith in children who have not developed sufficient adaptive brain functions. They will worry excessively when their children take charge of their own lives. The *Make-Sure Parents'* lack of faith will limit their ability to supply confidence for their children right when they need it most — when they encounter humbling and potentially traumatic failures.

Also, when parents do too much for their kids, they foster oppositionalism. And when children enter oppositional states, those *make-sure* points become *Hotspots* of conflict.

How Children Exploit Make-Sure Parents

Those with AD/HD and other behavorial problems discover how their *Make-Sure Parents* have a mission to protect and teach them no matter what their behavior. They sense the pressures brought upon their parents by the Wheel of Life. As soon as children make these discoveries, they tend to exploit them, and turn them to their own advantage. Having realized that their parents will invariably take care of everything, they learn to live mindlessly. They realize that the more irresponsibly they behave, the more ardently their parents will work to solve their problems and gratify their desires. In short, the less they think, the more they force their parents to think.

This realization frees AD/HD and other misbehaving children to pursue immediate gratification goals, whatever the cost. Exploiting the two commandments of parenting, these children become masters at a game of defiance I call *Control Poker*. Although no money is on the table, the stakes of Control Poker are high indeed. For in this game of winner-take-all, the children play for power.

A Quick Hand of Control Poker

See if this sounds familiar: You open the game by asking your child for obedience — in the kindest possible tone. "OK, sweetie, time to take a bath and get ready for bed." Faced with the choice of either obeying or ignoring, your child invariably chooses to ignore you, not even looking up from the Nintendo screen. You then repeat your command three, five, even ten times. But your child still ignores you. (Neurological factors in AD/HD children make it unlikely that they will inconvenience themselves just to gain your approval. This is especially true when control is on the line.)

As your child continues to ignore your opening moves, including appeals for harmony between you, and offers of praise and affection, your frustration leads you to employ increasingly harsher tones. Like the former Boston Red Sox slugger Ted Williams, patiently fouling off pitch after pitch until he sees the one he wants to hit over the fence, your child waits out all your sweet requests until the punitiveness in your voice reaches a peak of urgency.

Just before you explode, your child smoothly defuses you with an appeal to the second commandment of parenting, your mission to educate your child. "But Mo-om,"or, "But Da-ad," your child whines, "why do I have to?" In asking why, he deftly shifts the conflict from the issue of disobedience to a philosophical argument. In compliance with the second commandment of parenting, you want your child to understand your reasons. So you attempt to explain. You may employ any or all of these arguments:

"You've been playing outside all day and you got pretty dirty. So now its time to clean up."

"Remember, you promised you'd be good when I bought you that toy you wanted."

"Your favorite TV show is on in half an hour. If you don't get ready for bed now, you'll miss it."

"You asked to join the soccer team and you have practice tomorrow morning."

For the sake of gaining even a momentary indulgence, your child will then seize upon one of the reasons offered and shred it. "Oh, that toy stinks: It doesn't do any of the stuff you see it do in the commercials." "I hate that show; it's totally lame." "I don't want to go to stupid soccer practice anyway." Now, instead of battling over the question of obedience, your child has you debating the merits of the toy, the TV show, or soccer. Your child's strategy is simple, even obvious. If he disagrees with your reasoning — and don't doubt for a second that he will disagree — Voila! he no longer needs to obey you. Indeed, disobedience becomes the only "logical" course of action. "So why can't I take my bath later?"

As you attempt to reason with your child, he may interrupt your flow with whiny appeals to your nurturing, protective side. "Do I have to take a bath? Pleeeeeease!" Although these appeals for your "kindness," in reality, your surrender, lack sincerity, the tone sends the message: "Please spare me this severe pain. Aren't you tired yet? We don't have to keep doing this, you know." This strategy is calculated to wear you down — and often is effective.

By now, you are exasperated and bewildered. If your child had only taken a bath the first time you asked, you'd both be finished already.

Yet, neither you nor your child may be ready to quit. Your child has two reasons to continue waging the battle. First, he wants to demonstrate that he has control. But this struggle for control points to a second reason. Your child's pride is invested in the outcome of this game of Control Poker. Unable to build pride and self-esteem through achievements of his own, your child boosts his ego through his victories over you. By now, you may feel thoroughly caught up in the effort to determine the outcome of this contest of wills. Your child's apparent uninvolvement in the game (a good poker face) draws you in deeper, making you more impassioned about winning the game. After eight gentle requests, one angry command and an exhausting debate, you move on to threats.

"If you don't get up to the tub right now, I'll take your Nintendo and throw it in the trash!" Unimpressed, your child may stick with the same strategy, asking yet again, "Why?" Or he may counter with his own threats. "You do and I won't go to school anymore! Ever! And you can't make me!" Your child may even decide this is the time to use his ace in the hole: threats of self-injury. Since they are in conflict with the first commandment of parenting ("Thou shalt protect thy child."), such threats as, "I'm going to run away from home, "or "I'm going to kill myself," are virtually unbeatable cards in Control Poker.

Eventually, once the coercive cycle of the game of Control Poker has begun, you will have to choose one of three alternatives: acquiesce to your child's stubborness, use physical force, or punish. Each inflicts its own particular damage on both you and your child. Those who ultimately acquiesce often do so with a bitter remark, such as, "Fine, stay dirty, stink up the place for all I care." Not only does such a comment negate you by denying the importance of what you want your child to do, and falsely implying that you no longer care for your child, but it wounds your child, as well. At the same time, such acquiescence reinforces the dysfunctional patterns of family interaction and the child's control over you.

Those who finally resort to physical force by, for example, carrying a kicking, screaming, biting, hitting child to the bathroom, tearing off the child's clothes, and dumping him into the bathtub, end up with something worse than a flooded bathroom floor. Everyone involved feels demeaned by the experience. Your child, who invests so much pride in issues of control, feels severely diminished, his self-esteem damaged even further. And no matter how justified you feel at the moment, you also feel profoundly guilty afterward for physically overpowering him in a direct violation of the commandment to "protect thy child."

Those who administer punishments in anger and frustration often go overboard: "Fine, don't get ready for bed. But you're grounded tomorrow. And if you say one more word, I'll ground you for a week." This ending only lays the groundwork for future trouble. The punishment will probably end up serving as just another source of defiance, conflict, and coercion — another round of Control Poker.

In this situation, your child counts on getting out of the punishment, and chalks up another victory. The child understands that you're worn out for now, and that later you will feel badly. If you do not rescind the punishment yourself, your child will no doubt use it to start another game of Control Poker. Often, the guilt that both you and your child feel prompts a reconciliation, an agreement to forget the whole thing. You may do something special together to cement the reconciliation. Thus, not only has the child won the round of Control Poker, but he gets this additional treat of something special as "icing on the cake." Dr. Russell Barkley, the most esteemed proponent of behaviorist approaches to AD/HD, has shown that, since, in essence, the "something special" rewards defiance, this type of reconciliation reinforces antisocial behavior. Indeed, no professional could design a better training program to promote defiance.

To sum it up, once you have entered into a game of Control

Poker with your child, you cannot win. If you use physical force, you damage your child's self-esteem, and some of your own as well. If you acquiesce or impose punishment, your child knows he has won for now. "Wow," your child thinks, breathing a sigh of relief and returning to whatever he was doing before the incident began. "Good game!"

In the movie *War Games*, the young hero uses the game of tic-tac-toe to teach an advanced military computer an important lesson about nuclear war: The only winning move is not to play the game. Just so with Control Poker. If you allow yourself to be drawn into a game, you've already lost. The next chapter considers what would happen if you dropped your *make-sure* role, put your child in charge of key obligations, and allowed him to take responsibility for the consequences of not cooperating.

3 The Natural-Consequences Attitude

This chapter will introduce you to a missing ingredient in much of the parenting technology available today — Attachment Theory. Attachment Theory explains irrational actions of humans. It makes these understandable and predictable, something behavioral and learning theories struggle to comprehend. Much of the interaction involved in parenting and other intimate relationships is mediated by the attachment brain. Thus, the best way to understand the phenomena involved is from the perspective of Attachment Theory.

The story behind this influential theory begins with an unlikely experiment conducted a half century ago. Conrad Lorenz won a Nobel Prize for his experiments in the early 1900s on the imprinting, or bonding, process of ducklings. He found that ducklings who were exposed to surrogate mothers during an initial critical period subsequently preferred these objects over their biological mothers. Some of these surrogates were inanimate objects, like a football, or a wire-mesh approximation of a duck, with feathers glued to it. Lorenz observed how, once bonded, these ducklings followed the object of attachment blindly. Thus, we learned two fundamental properties of the attachment brain: (1) loyalty, and (2) the pursuit of sameness, which involves constancy and repetition.

Lorenz made another critical observation. He varied the speed at which the ducklings had to pursue the surrogate mothers. He found an amazing correlation between how hard the mother was to keep up with, and how strong the bond became. The ducklings worked extremely hard and became very clingy to the harder-to-get mothers. Thus, we learned another fundamental property of the attachment brain: attraction and devotion will increase when objects are hard to get.

Scientists have demonstrated varying levels of the same process operating in different mammals. Zebras, for example, display almost the same imprinting characteristics as ducklings, except they are programmed to bond to stripe patterns. They form an irreversible bond to the first adult zebra they see, recognizing their primary object of attachment by the adult's distinct stripe patterns. Once bonded, they will follow this adult zebra, usually the mother, with unceasing loyalty, into the harshest of conditions, even unto death. There is nothing rational about the attachment process. The properties of the attachment brain remain the same: a predictable sense of consistency, loyalty and devotion, and an intensification of these properties in response to objects that are hard to get.

Lorenz's work on attachment was eventually generalized to humans, and gave birth to Attachment Theory, a very credible and promising school of thought within psychology. Key figures like Bowlby led the efforts to understand the attachment process in human development. Psychoanalytic theories like Object Relations and Self Theory have relied heavily on constructs from Attachment Theory, and used these to explain our tendency to repeat irrational behavior, and response to trauma. Neurobiological theories have confirmed the presence and functions of an attachment brain in humans.

Investigators today are conducting important studies in which they provide good-quality attachments in early childhood in populations at high risk for delinquency. They are finding solid evidence that meeting early attachment needs helps form a healthy conscience, which brings with it the capacity for concern. It is believed that this kind of attachment experience can avert the development of antisocial and violent behavior later in life in at least a significant portion of the population.

The following section of this book simplifies the explanation of Attachment Theory by pointing out the similarity between the laws of magnetism, and the fundamental properties of relationships. It also discusses the *Natural-Consequences Attitude*, which derives from Attachment Theory all the elements necessary to free you from the *make-sure* parenting trap.

Attract, Repel: The Key to the Right Attitude

In elementary school we learned that opposite poles of two magnets attract, while like poles repel each other. Our observation of the attachment process similarly holds that the emotional tone or behavior that one person adopts will elicit the opposite tone or behavior from the other person. For example, parents who give tirelessly and without limits create a magnetic pull for their children to take ravenously, and yet remain dissatisfied. Parents who worry excessively are encouraging their children to be rash and reckless. Those who take an overly-active role in their children's lives pull for passivity in their children. Controlling parents pull for rebellious children. Most sadly, parental abuse, ironically, and all too often, results in children who cling desperately to their parents.

Attachment Theory also holds that the more extreme the stance taken by, say, a parent, the more magnetic the charge will be — that is, the greater the force that will be exercised to produce the opposite stance in the child. So the more protective a parent becomes, the greater the likelihood the child will be destructive and heedless of danger. The more ambitious a parent becomes regarding the child, the greater the risk that the child will lose interest in achievement.

For our purposes, it is better to adopt a mild rather than an extreme magnetic stance. Extreme stances pull for extreme reactions, carrying with them the risk of trauma and other unhealthy consequences. You will derive the most from Attachment Theory by making for your child the privilege of your presence, attention, and help moderately hard to get.

Playing Hard to Get

Almost everyone has either seen or experienced the magnetic properties of relationships. At some point in our lives, most of us have felt the appeal and pull of someone who played "hard to get." Maybe the guy who sat two seats in front of you in high school biology. Or perhaps the woman who lived across the hall the first time you had an apartment of your own.

Those who play hard to get are often mesmerizing, drawing us toward them as they push us away. They seem so playful, so fun-loving, yet, at the same time, too busy with their own lives and their other friends to give us the attention we so passionately desire. They never seem to want to take charge of the situation, or of us. They don't put any effort into building a relationship with us. So we try to take charge. We do all the work. We turn ourselves inside out trying to start conversations, make phone calls, ask for dates.

Small successes often reward our pursuits of those who are hard to get. She returns one of your calls. Or he agrees to meet you for lunch. But each occasional triumph inevitably is followed by silence, distance, or excuse for not getting together again because, it appears, of a prior commitment. Yet, somehow, this apparent lack of interest, especially when it is coupled with the occasional tiny victory, only compels us to try even harder, to make ourselves even more appealing. And as long as our effort continues to reap any kind of reward, no matter how small, we feel happy about ourselves and what we are doing. This kind of relationship may be hard to get, but it is not unhealthy.

The Coaching Role

High school athletic coaches also illustrate the magnetic properties of human aattachment. The fun and excitement of the sports they coach induce among students a desire to be part of the team. Yet, at the same time, they present kids with a challenge, because trying out for the team does not guarantee making the team.

Coaches become magnetic by being close enough to attract, but simultaneously maintaining a certain distance from their players. Even if they want a particular person to be part of the team, they don't need any one player, no matter how good. Those who don't try hard enough, who refuse to put the team's interests above their own, will be benched or dropped in favor of others who do. Coaches insist that the same rules apply to everyone, and require all of their players to do the work needed to stay on the team. As long as the coach gives all players a chance to show what they can do, this hard-to-get relationship not only remains healthy, but actually promotes self-improvement. Each individual works to make the team grow in strength, skill, and confidence.

Your Child's Magnetic Appeal

Coaches and others who play hard to get in a healthy way follow the same pattern in demonstrating their magnetism. A lure — something the other person wants — attracts the other person's interest, desire, or ambition. Yet, the other person has to work hard in order to achieve a thrilling moment of success. And each success is followed by still another challenge.

You may not realize the extent to which your child has exercised just such a magnetic influence on you. Your child, no matter how difficult, has an undeniable and immeasurable appeal to you. He has something you want — behavior that will make him healthy and successful in life. Yet, your difficult child plays hard to get, seldom allowing you even a small triumph, a brief moment of success, the fleeting satisfaction of being a good parent. As parents, we end up caught in an unhealthy hard-to-get relationship (unhealthy because it offers no fair return for your efforts), and, as a result, may feel despair and become depressed. As your child becomes more and more difficult, increasingly uncooperative and demanding, you have to work overtime to achieve even a little bit of gratification. Driving home from what has been for you an exhausting day at the amusement park, you find your child already complaining of boredom and begging to be taken to the mall. No sooner does your child finish a double-scoop hot fudge sundae than he wants you to buy some candy. Because AD/HD allows satisfaction only for the moment, your child never stops asking for more. Typically, AD/HD children do not work to gratify their own desires; instead, they rely on their parents or siblings to jump through hoop after hoop for them.

Brian, thirteen, had his family bending over backward trying to satisfy his desires. Brian would begin by whining for whatever he wanted: something sweet to eat, the hottest video game or latest CD. When his parents gave him what he wanted, he had to have more. And the more his parents gave him, the more abusive he became. The abuse escalated until finally, in trying to force his mother to give him what he wanted, he broke her arm.

When children, in effect, borrow their parents' frontal lobes, they avoid the exercise of vital mental functions, and, consequently, their frontal lobes atrophy. As the parent of an AD/HD or otherwise difficult child, you face painful choices. Should you continue to micromanage your child's daily routine, operating as his cognitive crutch in a pattern which may yield immediate gratification and provide safety for your child, but, in the long run, will induce boredom, laziness, despotism and weakness? Or should you remove the safety net, a strategy which may involve some initial failure and pain, but, in the long run, will mature and strengthen your child?

Reversing the Polarities

Although most people find it easier to resist change than to embrace it, choosing the first alternative will worsen your child's AD/HD symptoms, and leave you locked in the dysfunctional patterns that AD/HD has created in your family. Left to their own devices, these difficult children will hold out for their parents and siblings to do all the work, in an unhealthy, hard-to-get relationship. When they don't get what they want, AD/HD children tend to: (1) avoid thought, (2) lack motivation, (3) demand constant attention, and (4) wreak havoc on the family. These children have been magnetically pulling for extraordinary amounts of protection, thinking, work, favors, and conflict.

In advocating the second alternative — removal of the safety net — I hope to reverse the polarities of the magnetic relationship between you and your child — and thereby avoid the Control Poker trap. The *Natural-Consequences Attitude* puts the magnetic properties of Attachment Theory to practical use. Since the problems between you and your difficult child probably center in your over-attachment, and the struggle for control, both Attachment Theory and common sense dictate that you detach, put some distance between yourself and your child, and give up any illusions of control. The *Natural-Consequences Attitude* not only establishes this distance, but allows you to become a magnet for your child, instead of the reverse. By establishing a healthy hard-to-get relationship, you can foster the kinds of behavior and attitude you want your child to develop.

The key elements of this magnetic strategy include: (1) possession by you of something your child wants, including your attention and family privileges; (2) self-satisfaction on your part, or the ability to seem content and busy with your own life without your child's cooperation, the opposite of the *Make-Sure Parenting* role; (3) the setting up of challenges for your child; and (4) letting your child do the work in the relationship, but permitting him a sense of victory, and giving evidence of your appreciation of his labors, thus promoting an atmosphere of fair give-and-take.

By adopting a consistent *Natural-Consequences Attitude* position, you can reverse the polarities of the defiant relationship. By attaching playfully to your child, you will exert a magnetic pull for the development of his own ambition and desire for attachment. By remaining playful, you will buffer the consequences of your child's encounters with reality after he begins to manage his own affairs. By remaining unhelpful, you will pull for your child to begin exercising vital *make-sure* functions. By insisting that your child earn privileges and possessions, you will pull for the child's gratitude. By giving up control and responsibility, you will pull for your child to become more responsible. In time, your difficult child will become more cooperative and better motivated.

Does this sound far-fetched? If it does, think of the dynamics in many alcoholic households. For nearly two decades, family therapists have recognized that children of alcoholics often become "parentified." Since alcoholics and their co-dependent spouses seldom take appropriate responsibility for their households or their children, the children themselves often begin to take on adult, or parental, responsibilities, meanwhile feeling emotionally neglected. This phenomenon, however, can have positive effects in a relationship with a defiant child. Combined with emotional presence and a playful attitude, a calculated degree of parental "irresponsibility" stimulates responsibility in children in accordance with the principle of magnetism.

The *Natural-Consequences Attitude* depends on this combination of playful emotional presence and non-helpful stance, in which parents refuse to assume the *make-sure* role and take over responsibility from the child, or to shield the child from consequences of his actions.

Betty and Gerard were skeptical when they first considered adopting a *Natural-Consequences Attitude* with their thirteen-year-old son, Jerry. Every day they would battle to get him ready for the school bus. They were convinced that if they didn't drag him out of bed in the morning, nag him to dress, and sit him down to breakfast he would never get to school, at all. But they decided to give the *Natural-Consequences Attitude* a try.

One evening, they told Jerry that from now on he'd have to get himself ready in time for the bus. The next morning Jerry overslept as usual, no doubt having gone to sleep believing his parents would wake him in time for school. Betty, who runs a small business from her home, occupied herself with paperwork and various other tasks instead of trying to rouse Jerry, as was her custom in the past. By the time he woke up on his own, it was too late for him to catch the bus. Betty good-naturedly made it clear that, despite whatever entreaties might develop, she would not be available for school transportation before 9:45, and then for only the next fifteen minutes. This was almost two hours after the start of classes. Still too late for the bus, and ignored by his mother, Jerry filled in the time at home for the next few days by watching TV, including a morning sports roundup. This was fun for a while, but the novelty soon wore off. Jerry became anxious about being late for school, and tried calling friends for rides. But this didn't work. Betty, supported by Gerard, stuck to her guns, and drove her son to school only on the basis of her own timetable.

Betty and Gerard buffered the consequences to Jerry and the school by meeting with Jerry's teachers and the school administrators to explain the situation. The school staff understood, adopted a reasonable attitude, and dispensed sensible consequences. It was now up to Jerry himself to make sure he reached school on time. Betty and Gerard remained committed to this experiment, and persisted with the *Natural-Consequences Attitude*. And it worked. After little more than a week of tardiness, of falling behind in his assignments, and of sensing that his popularity at the school had declined, Jerry assumed responsibility for getting himself ready in the morning. Since then, he has not missed the school bus once.

From the standpoint of the Attachment Theory, the *Natural-Consequences Attitude* can best be summarized as the reverse of the overprotection you may now be lavishing upon your difficult child. It means permitting your child, within certain safety parameters, to experience the results of irresponsible behavior, and the disappointments of failure as well as the thrill of success. Although you remain interested in and supportive of your child's decisions, you cannot allow yourself to interfere with the outcome. This is the most critical — and most difficult — aspect of the *Natural-Consequences Attitude*.

To help your child move beyond the self-centeredness and impulsiveness that AD/HD prolongs, you will need to redirect your relationships with him, taking a more nonprotective attitude. This means no longer spoiling your child with either material objects, or with lavish efforts directed toward satisfying — or trying to satisfy — his needs and solving his problems. The *Natural-Consequences Attitude* calls on you as a parent to adopt an approach involving (1) minimal assistance in answer to his needs; (2) an increased air of self-importance, an attitude that tells the child you don't want him on your side if he won't contribute to your happiness; and (3) playfulness when you demonstrate admiration of your child's efforts, good or bad. This takes the edge off the consequences, and reduces the likelihood of their becoming traumatic.

You have probably noticed a similarity between the attitudes and behaviors I ask you to adopt and those of your AD/HD child, himself. These include not thinking for the other person, not helping, and demanding loyalty. If you consider Attachment Theory, you will realize why. By applying the theory in this way, you will bring about a degree of role reversal as you exert a magnetic pull for your child to think for himself, help himself, and work toward achieving the things that he wants.

This reversal of roles, however, is not complete: playfulness and fair payback provide the difference. For both you and your child, playfulness reduces the harshness of the battle for power in which you both are engaged. Playfulness also creates the state of mind you need to cheer your child on as he struggles to succeed. In addition, playfulness allows you to maintain a connection with what's going on in the struggle, and to avoid complete separation from events.

One of the fundamental elements of play involves pretending. Deep down, you aren't really unhelpful, involved only in yourself. If your child makes a genuine effort and still needs your help or your intellect, you will be available and willing to provide them. But if your child can succeed, even partially, on his own, you can help most by simply letting the child achieve his own triumphs, and then applauding what he did.

My Child, Right or Wrong

The *Natural-Consequences Attitude* will free you to create a new, supportive, and affectionate relationship with your difficult child. Before, your most determined efforts to educate your child always ended up in nagging, lectures, and scolding. With all the fighting, you probably had little chance to show your child the affection you feel for him. By giving up your overprotective involvement in the outcome of your child's actions, you allow the world at large to fashion the consequences and teach the lessons your child needs to learn. Playfully attached to your child means playfully detached from the controlling *Make-Sure Parenting* role. Now you can offer your support and affection without emotional complications.

The *Natural-Consequences Attitude* thus allows you to form a positive bond with your anti-discipline, and sometimes negative, child. Your child won't do what you or his teachers ask? Fine. Agree with him that the task or chore is stupid, that discipline is difficult, that it's much more fun to escape responsibilities than to meet them. Suggest that consequences will sooner or later teach him why this selfishness will cause more trouble than it's worth, and project, at the same time, a "you'll see" attitude, with an air of confidence. By identifying with your child's rebellion against discipline, you take his side.

How can you bring yourself to condone, much less applaud, your child's defiance? A commitment to the *Natural-Consequences Attitude* begins with the recognition that engaging in round after round of Control Poker in attempts to command obedience does not work with unruly children, and especially with those who have AD/HD. As you have seen, pitting yourself against your child inflicts damage on both of you. Control Poker casts you in the role of your child's most formidable adversary. The *Natural-Consequences Attitude*, on the other hand, establishes you as your child's strongest and most supportive ally.

The key to this strategy is in how you choose to characterize your child's response to your calls for obedience. If your child defies you, you need to consider that behavior as tricky or clever, rather than as bad. You don't state this out loud, however. You think it. Your attitude is implied in your behavior. If your child complies, you need to think of that compliance as evidence of maturity. Either way, your child's response does not affect your stance: you're on your child's side.

Granted that this goes against the traditional model of *Make-Sure Parenting*. Traditional parents yield to society's expectations in attempting to win compliance from their children. They try to harness their children's willfulness and selfishness, and to foster self-discipline by citing the interests of others. They emphasize the Golden Rule, "Do unto others as you would have them do unto you." Yet, children with AD/HD, because of their neurological impairment, cannot make this profound leap. The traditional parenting model defines the child who complies as "good." If a child deviates or rebels against compliance and discipline, however, the child is "bad," the child's behavior is "naughty," and the child's emotions are "negative." Yet, with AD/HD and other difficult children such punitive-type evaluations and remarks frequently trigger the coercive cycle of Control Poker.

By contrast, the *Natural-Consequences Attitude* appeals to the child's self-interest in order to cultivate pride. Although you identify with and allow your child's rebellion, at the same time you establish a clear limit. Your child's pain and dislikes do not excuse irresponsible behavior. No, not in YOUR family! You need to show your child that noncompliance comes at a price. This means not shielding your child from the consequences of noncompliance or antisocial behavior directed toward teachers or others. And it means consistently and playfully enforcing the consequences of defiance in the home. If the child won't do what's needed to contribute to family life, for example, that's his choice. But you will dispense consequences. He can't expect to share in the power, privileges, and fun of the family.

Taking advantage of the magnetic properties of human attachment, the *Natural-Consequences Attitude* uses the lure and power of the peer world to obtain the desired behavior from misbehaving children. Making family support for these activities desirable and accessible, but, at the same time, "hard to get" maximizes the appeal of family membership. The child finds out that he must be a team player to share in the power and privileges that come with being part of the family.

Think back to the magnetic appeal exercised by the coach of the sports team. Good coaches demand a contributory, team-based attitude, and a certain level of discipline and effort from all of their players. The best coaches de-emphasize winning and losing, success and failure. They stress attitude, effort, and performing up to the limit of one's capabilities. The desired results will follow. Finally, win or lose, skilled coaches give proper credit not to their own coaching, but to the effort and performance of the players. As you assume the role of coach in your family, you too will need to exemplify these virtues.

To draw the child toward desirable behavior, the family must adopt a magnetic stance – the *Natural-Consequences Attitude*. You and the other family members, including your spouse and your other children, must appear content without the company of your problem child when he is not contributing. Soon, your child will come asking you to restore privileges — and be willing to do all the work necessary to rejoin the family. The price of admission will be reparation: a demonstration of respect for family, and for the privileges the child has misused. In this way, the *Natural-Consequences Attitude* is actually a positive attachment, a magnetic stance that exerts its pull for the development of your child's self-esteem. The *Natural-Consequences Attitude* promotes the development of *make-sure* abilities in children. The following describes how this process takes place.

The Role of Separation Anxiety

Separation anxiety results when a child must confront a challenging situation without the presence of a parental figure. Separation anxiety is prominent and terrifying in early childhood. As children mature, they develop a sense of parental presence that allows them to function even when the parent is not present physically. Children need to believe in a parental presence that protects them when it is needed, anticipates difficulties, and bails them out of trouble.

Parents spare their children a great deal of worry by keeping track of their overwhelming heap of obligations. Children sense their parents' involvement in their business, and live as though these worries didn't exist. Parental worry provides a priceless sense of security for young children. And the children always take this support for granted. They have no way of appreciating the weight these worries place on their parents. Children will not exercise their own abilities to manage these affairs as long as they sense that their parents will do the job for them.

The relationship between childhood needs and parental worry

is parasitic, a link between the child's attachment system and the parent's adaptive brain. The child provides the functions of the attachment brain, which involve the expression of needs. The adult provides the complementary functions of the adaptive brain, which involve all the *make-sure* functions required to manage these affairs, and ultimately gratify the child's needs.

Separation anxiety signals to the child's adaptive brain that it must mobilize all necessary *make-sure* functions to discharge an obligation, even if this means relying on its own inferior resources. In the absence of parental *make-sure* functions, the child senses a threat to survival. A child in this situation will need to summon up the necessary *make-sure* functions for himself. The process can be likened to how hospital ICUs turn to emergency back-up generators, but only in the event of main power outages.

Parents who will not even allow themselves to think about their children's specific obligations will set the stage for sufficient separation anxiety to trigger exercise of *make-sure* abilities in the child. In a state of disbelief, the child will initially view failure as something that is not happening. The child will soon, however, expect and demand parental rescue. Yet, he will take complete charge of the situation once the parent resists the urge to comply. Children, in fact, will take tremendous pride in the quality of their accomplishments once they have mastered particular obligations. Each obligation shifted to the child this way will constitute a unit of maturation.

Parents who make the mistake of dedicating themselves to relieving their children of separation anxiety will constantly provide *make-sure* functions for them. As a result, their children will fail to mature. They will take the parents' efforts for granted, and become exceedingly demanding. They will become accustomed to the parasitic relationship, confident that they possess tremendous adaptive abilities, yet unable to perform even adequate *make-sure* functions for themselves. They will become oppositional in response to help they no longer require. Yet, these children will change dramatically in response to the *Natural-Consequences Attitude*.

Many children who have been extremely uncooperative when their parents have been "the boss" will become extremely dutiful when they become their own bosses. Parents often are dumbfounded when their nightmare of a child suddenly becomes highly dedicated, and sets the highest of standards for himself. I am no longer surprised to see this turn of events. Difficult children tend to become very responsive to their own parental instincts once their real-life parents drop their old *make-sure* roles.

Kate had been told that Paul, her eleven-year-old AD/HD son, was biologically incapable of managing basic obligations, like getting up in the morning, going to bed at night, sitting down to do homework, or occupying himself in play activities to overcome boredom. Kate assumed that Paul lacked the organizational abilities to clean his own room, and accepted him as a casualty of AD/ HD. As a result of her assumption, Kate literally had become Paul's servant. She did everything for him, and yet he became abusive when things didn't turn out exactly as he wanted.

After attending a parenting class, however, Kate decided to follow the program I have outlined in this book, and one day informed Paul that he would be in charge of getting himself out of bed and ready for the school bus in the morning. Paul predictably went right back to sleep after his first and only wake-up call. The time was 6:15 a.m. It was 6:55 when Kate heard a shriek of panic, and the stream of insults pouring out of Paul's room:

"I can't believe you didn't wake me up!"

"How dare you do this to me! . . . I hate you!"

"I'm going to get into so much trouble."

"This is so embarrassing!"

"I can't believe you didn't wake me up! . . ."

The tantrum went on for quite some time, with random accusations, and declarations of hatred and intent to do harm, mixed with self-pity.

Paul's separation anxiety had kicked in. It had taken fifty minutes. Kate didn't say much. Both felt sick in the stomach for a few hours. Kate attempted to buffer the trauma for Paul by writing him an excuse to give to the teacher. But this didn't console Paul very much. The embarrassment of being late to school obviously had a much greater impact on Paul than any consequences that could be devised.

The next morning Kate overslept. She felt so guilty. It was 6:40 a.m., and Paul would have to experience separation anxiety once more. She stumbled to his room in a state of disarray, moving from drowsiness to panic. Much to Kate's surprise, Paul was not in his bed. She looked around aimlessly for a while before he sprang out from a hiding-place behind an open door. Laughing, teasing, rambunctious, he was fully dressed and ready for school, with shoes, coat and backpack on.

That afternoon Kate reminded Paul that he was to do his homework before going out to play. Paul lied, and announced he had no homework. Kate offered tutoring support for the next hour, in case there was homework, but declared herself off duty after 6 p.m. Paul wanted to go out and play before the sun went down, so he passed on the tutoring. Later that night, Paul was nowhere to be found. Kate and her husband finally discovered him hiding in a corner of his room, secretly working on his homework. In a throwback to the old days, Kate's husband wanted to ground Paul for having lied. Kate, however, thought of another way to benefit from the incident — to separate herself from homework duty in the future. If Paul had come out of his room begging for help, she would have had him earn it with some kitchen work — in a kind of barter system. It turned out this wasn't necessary. Paul did all the work alone.

The amount of time it takes children to experience a healthy dose of separation anxiety and take charge of specific obligations will vary. Some children take an hour to do so, as in Paul's case. Others take months. It depends on the child's temperament and constitution, the extent to which the parents put the matter out of their minds, and the consequences the child anticipates facing if he fails to discharge his obligations. Nonetheless, separation anxiety will kick in sooner or later, certainly within a few months. The child will then take over obligations with pride, and the obligations will remain off the parents' plate for years to come.

The process of mastery can also take time to develop even after your child's own *make-sure* functions have taken over. Separation anxiety ensures the transfer of responsibility to the child's own adaptive brain. It ensures the exercise of vital *make-sure* functions. But it doesn't ensure success. The child must develop the abilities to master the challenge. This is why it is important to maintain reasonable expectations when allowing children to take charge and experience the consequences of their actions. It doesn't pay to establish expectations which exceed the ability of the child to fulfill.

My own AD/HD son was late thirty-six times in one semester before he developed sufficient separation anxiety to get up in the morning without assistance. However, he has gotten up like clockwork ever since that was achieved. The results have been lasting. My son, now a teenager, goes to bed at precise times. He may leave waffles in the toaster the night before. He goes through a precise ritual to balance his sleep and board the school bus by 7 a.m. He juggles numerous responsibilities in order to maintain a B-C average, have a social life, and play on the school basketball team. He relies on a sophisticated set of *make-sure* functions to determine when he must get up early, when he can be late, when he must study, and when he can allow himself to fail. It's his lifestyle. It's a hard one, and he takes pride in it.

The point of this section is that you can predict when your child will take over *make-sure* functions for a particular obligation. The answer lies in the extent of separation anxiety he exhibits once you decide to get the obligation "off your plate." You will allow your child to take over responsibility for a series of obligations, and make a genuine effort not to worry about these. Your child will initially fail to exercise the necessary *make-sure* functions, and will seem doomed to fail. However, the threat of mounting consequences will sooner or later trigger the necessary separation anxiety, and your child's own adaptive brain will allocate the resources to perform the necessary *make-sure* functions. Your child will master the task, mature, and derive a strong sense of pride from the experience.

It is important to emphasize that expectations must be reasonable for this kind of growth to take place, and the child must face sensible consequences for misusing privileges or failing to take responsibility. Adopting a *Natural-Consequences Attitude* alone would be wrong and insufficient.

My formula for fostering natural development in children involves meeting vital attachment needs while challenging adaptive brain functions. In the next chapter, you will learn how to produce the splendor of natural development in your children by surrounding them with consequences that teach and strengthen. This will supplement your *Natural-Consequences Attitude,* and free you once and for all from the perils of *Make-Sure Parenting.*

4 Consequences That Teach and Strengthen

Behavior modification specializes in the technology of consequences. It addresses the needs of the adaptive brain like no other theory can. Behavior modification limits its focus to antecedents and consequences — what precedes and follows a given behavior, and to how organisms change their outward behavior in response to manipulations of these two external forces. Behavior modification is a very important theory to consider. However, it is misunderstood and misused all too often.

We are all victims of our assumptions, and behavior modification is no exception. Our assumptions organize and clarify our perceptions, but also cause our blind spots. We all fail to see information that differs from our assumptions. Behavior modification is blinded by an assumption called the *black box*. The black box represents the internal processes of the organism behaviorists seek to change. The black box theorem states that one cannot measure what goes on inside an organism, and, therefore, one should dismiss this potential source of information as nonscientific and invalid.

This self-imposed limitation of behavior modification came about in response to the speculation going on at the time in psychoanalytic circles. Nothing psychoanalysts speculated about could be challenged, yet they speculated about everything from penis envy, cigars, and anal fixations, to castration anxiety, reaction formation and polymorphous perversion. Psychoanalytic theory could not be refuted, because it had an exception for every one of its rules. Therefore, if the theory made an erroneous prediction, the discrepancy would be classified as one of its recognized exceptions, and the observation was still thought to support the theory.

Behavior modification's disinterest in what goes on inside the organism cost it the benefits of major breakthroughs, including temperament, the attachment system's influence on irrational behavior, developmental states, the role of trauma, and biochemical imbalances, to name a few. Behavior modification could be applied indiscriminately to a child, dog or rat. It has been used successfully to train pigeons to fly missiles into enemy targets, housebreak dogs, and cure people of phobias.

In recent years, behavior modification has aligned itself with Cognitive Learning Theory to compensate for its black box limitation. Cognitive behavior modification addresses the thought processes that take place inside the organism, that black box. However, behavior modification often ends up considering only Learning Theory, failing to account for the source of all persistent irrational behavior — Attachment Theory. This makes it blind to the control problem of the *Make-Sure Parent*, among other things.

In this chapter, we will borrow the best that behavior modification has to offer for dispensing effective consequences. We will supplement it with important elements from other theories to compensate for its limitations and misuse. We will utilize it to strengthen brain functions in your AD/HD child. This section will prepare you to employ consequences to shape your children's behavior in a way that will foster growth.

The Active Ingredient in Time Out

I will begin this section by introducing the active ingredient behind all the interventions you will learn. A true understanding of the psychology that makes consequences effective will put you in a position to appreciate their unique role in your children's development, and allow you to implement them with confidence and peace of mind. You've probably used the fundamental principles involved in these consequences countless times. You have if you've ever used *Time Out*.

Time Out is by far the most effective and widely accepted psychological tool for child-rearing ever devised. The active ingredient in Time Out is the removal of relationships and family privileges for having misused them. If you stop to think about it, when children are in Time Out, they lose having a Mom, a Dad, siblings, access to certain privileges, and involvement in family activities. Some leading versions of Time Out allow children to remain in a room with toys and stimulating objects. The loss of family involvement effectively stops disruptive behavior, without recourse to punitive measures like isolation. Loss of belonging is a powerful consequence.

The key to administering the right consequences is in having them simulate real life. We want consequences that teach the right lessons, are strong enough to shape your child, yet modest enough to prevent harm. Time Out achieves this. It simulates the natural consequence that occurs in real life as a result of destructive behavior. When you violate the rights of others, you lose them for yourself. Time Out has a decisive impact, and causes no harm.

Time Out robs oppositional children of their energy. Children borrow energy from those around them to fuel their tantrums. It is very hard to maintain a tantrum when no one is around to appreciate it. The key to dealing with tantrums is to remove the privilege of your presence. In Time Out, your child misuses a relationship, temporarily loses it, has a tantrum that runs its course, and then becomes appreciative.

Time Out was designed to meet the needs of the oppositional phase of development. Parents play a twofold role when dealing with oppositional children by (1) providing them with non-belonging, which is temporary isolation, and (2) allowing them to fail, while, at the same time, remaining confident in their ability to outgrow this phase of development. Time Out separates children from their families. It teaches the child the essential lesson that oppositional behavior leads to misuse of privileges and causes failure. Failure comes with having stopped the conflict-laden activity. You can administer Time Out with full confidence that no harm will result.

The optimal Time Out utilizes the experience of being non-family in a constructive way. The Time Out is delivered primarily when children enter oppositional states, or selfishly misuse privileges. It is most productive when administered firmly, but with temperance, patience, a positive outlook, and respectful body language.

Extending Time Out to Older Children

When younger children violate the rights of others, they can be effectively managed with Time Out. They lose privileges for a few minutes, and regain them once they calm down and become appreciative. This is not, however, a practical or sufficient consequence for older children for several reasons. First, it can become physically impossible to carry a twelve-year-old to the place where he will spend his Time Out. Second, at certain stages in development, "doing time" by being separate from the family is not a meaningful consequence. Older children will actually welcome separation from their families while in their oppositional states. They will also, however, feel humiliated, and this will encourage rebellion. Time Out will not be sufficient to foster a change in their attitude toward the family. Doing time fails to approximate the real-life consequences that result from violating the rights of others. In real life, you may lose relationships. It will take reparative gestures to regain trust and friendship.

In this program, older children who fail to contribute to the family, or who violate the rights of others, will lose all the privileges of being part of the family — a state I call *Off Privileges*. The important lesson that comes from being Off Privileges is that your children will learn to appreciate what they may otherwise take for granted. These privileges are made clear and spelled out for them in a posted notice for all to see called *House Privileges* (**see samples in Appendix A**). House Privileges include all the benefits that come from being part of the family, among them TV, telephone, video games, play dates, transportation, and allowance.

Children remain Off Privileges until they have performed reparative activities for having violated the rights of others. They are not forced to demonstrate respectful use of privileges. They regain their privileges on their own initiative by completing the tasks assigned. The work assignments are either spelled out in a *Fairness List* (**see Appendix B**), if the offender has failed to keep up with responsibilities in the house, or in the form of a *Reparative Duty*, for more serious infractions impacting the family.

Reparative Duty will involve an assigned task that will compensate the family for the time wasted in dealing with misbehavior. Through the performance of positive behavior that corresponds to the negative, completion of the task will undo the damage done. The combination of compensation and undoing should involve approximately one and one-half times the amount of problems caused others. For example, a sibling that repeatedly fails to share, to the extent that he ruins the family atmosphere, will become "low man on the totem pole" of sharing for the rest of the afternoon in order to regain family privileges. This Reparative Duty serves to refocus his attitude to one of family first. The lesson is simple: *If you misuse a privilege, you lose it; if you respect it, you get it back.*

Allowing vs. Dispensing Consequences

To a certain extent, you will allow natural consequences to teach your children vital lessons in situations that occur outside the home. Situations involving consequences will occur in his personal life that will make your child stop and reflect on his behavior. In some cases, these natural consequences can teach and strengthen your child. However, if they are too harsh, they will have the opposite effect. Instead of teaching and strengthening, they will traumatize and debilitate. Sometimes you will have to buffer the consequences you see and are allowing to happen.

You will be dispensing consequences in situations that primarily impact your home. Since the world does not react to behavior that occurs in the privacy of your own home, you will have to dispense approximations of the natural consequences that result from misbehavior if you are to help your children learn from their mistakes. Children who encounter consequences in real life for behaving irresponsibly, but are granted immunity from similar consequences at home, will escape natural consequences for their actions by hiding from them at home. Vital *make-sure* abilities will fail to develop when there are insufficient consequences at home.

One Parent Protects, the Other Inoculates

Most of us have heard of someone like the uncle who catches a nephew smoking, and forces him to smoke the entire cigar. The nephew experiences the negative side of smoking, and literally gets sick of smoking. Children learn important lessons this way. Perhaps smoking is not the best example to use, but it illustrates an important child-rearing principle — Allowing a child first-hand experience of the negative consequences of unwise behavior, in controlled doses, inoculates against dangerous exposure to indulgence in those behaviors later on. Such uncles might also invite their nephews to try standing out in the rain or cold, staying out late, going hungry, eating huge amounts of candy, watching endless hours of TV. The theory is simple, let them get sick of it, and they develop an immunity to it.

Medical doctors refer to this process as inoculation. They inject their patients with carefully titrated doses of viruses so the immune system develops the ability to fight them. This protects patients from more dangerous exposures. The lesson is that exposure to unwise behaviors can foster wisdom, given the right circumstances.

The process of inoculation is appropriate when your child has developed his own problem behaviors, or has been introduced to them by peers. You should not, however, force an innocent child to eat candy or smoke cigars, for these are addictive substances. You never introduce problem behaviors. The best use of Inoculation Theory is when your child resists important help that can prevent hardship in life outside the home. When this rejection occurs, encourage your child to go ahead and try life without exercising important brain functions, and have him do so without compensating supports. Your child will tire of living that way, and either try to change himself, or seek help.

A simple way to describe the difference between *Make-Sure Parenting* and *Natural-Consequences Parenting* is to examine the manner in which the two types of parents strive to protect their children. The *make-sure* parent shelters children to keep them from experiencing hardships. This implies to society that the child has not been handicapped by disabilities like AD/HD. *Natural-conquences parents* strengthen by inoculation. They encourage exposure to doing things in ways that cause reasonable hardship. This says to society that the child began with some significant shortcomings, but has mastered them and matured.

Make-sure parents utilize behavior modification to protect their children. They manipulate consequences to shelter them from exposure to life's dangers, and to prevent experiences of failure. This philosophy fails in the long run because it requires that experienced, well-inoculated individuals surround the child to protect the him from exposure to life's more dangerous traps. This is not realistic. The unexposed and inexperienced child will sooner or later wander out into the world, vulnerable to all sorts of exposures. The likelihood of a harmful consequence is much greater under these conditions.

Natural-consequences parents inoculate effectively by putting their children in charge of their own affairs so that they feel responsible for the consequences of their behavior. The experience of doing things in wrong-headed ways will force children to own up to their weaknesses, and master them. For children to develop immunities to poor habits through inoculation, their exposures must be limited, and their unwise behavior must yield reasonable consequences. Allowing and dispensing the right consequence are vital to the inoculation and strengthening process.

This book will tell what you will need in order to surround your child with the consequences that will teach and strengthen him. But before that, to learn what can occur when you surround a child with the right blend of consequences, consider the case of Jimmy, a typical unmotivated teenager, who happens to suffer from AD/HD and other learning disabilities.

Surrounding Jimmy with the Right Consequences

After attending a parenting class, Jimmy's parents dropped their *Make-Sure Parenting* role in dealing with their fifteen-year-old son, despite his continued failures in school. When they began to focus on being more playful and less helpful, their struggles decreased almost immediately. Jimmy began to work harder on his learning problems in response to his parents' newly-adopted allow stance, and to the apparent decrease in their concern about his school life. Separation anxiety had set in, and within a few weeks his own adaptive brain had begun making sure that his responsibilities were met. The school, nevertheless, began recommending an alternative placement, a move which was undoubtedly called for. Meanwhile, there was more happiness in the home. Good feelings invited good behavior, and Jimmy was developing a sense of belonging, and a sense of pride.

Jimmy's parents made the following adjustments to help Jimmy mature in spite of his academic limitations:

1. They required more work from him around the house. They delegated more important responsibilities to him, and included him in important family decisions and projects. Many of these were interesting, and some were charitable. Jimmy was productive.

2. They emphasized the importance of respect and contribution to family over and above school work, and took the position that academic excellence is only one way to reach success in life. People who are mature, reliable, and capable of hard work can be successful without books.

3. The family eventually asked Jimmy to consider being fair to himself, and help himself to obtain a good education.

Respect for the family and pride in his abilities had been established. Laziness had been conquered. School had been made less urgent, less a source of anxiety. Now was the time to focus on making the best of Jimmy's abilities. The family asked him to consider doing his best in two courses that he respected. He had permission to fail the others, or not even attend them. Jimmy took up the challenge. He started to do more work, but only in classes in which he developed an interest.

Jimmy's family had dispensed consequences correctly in areas that impacted on parents and family directly. They had used their influence to make him a vital contributor to the family — get him to do chores, and discharge a variety of other important responsibilities. If he failed, he lost the familiar family privileges, including TV, stereo, video games, phone, computer, rides to activities, and companionship. He had to make good on his obligations, and show respect for family to regain the privileges. Among his obligations was to be a good big brother to his little sister, Janet. If he upset her unjustly, he lost family privileges, as the disruption impacted the entire family. He had to be a respectful big brother for an entire day to win back his privileges. On the basis of his improved attitude, Jimmy and Janet became genuine friends and enjoyed being together. The parents became Jimmy's friends and allies, and stopped making demands about school. This buffered the consequences suffered there, and reduced the likelihood of trauma for Jimmy.

Jimmy's family had allowed consequences in areas that primarily affected his life outside the home. They made the problems he encountered in school and peer life his own to solve. They also made many of his responsibilities at home his own problems, as well. Jimmy had to wake up by himself, get himself to bed, clean his room, do his own laundry, and do his own homework. All of this was "off their plates"as parents. This had the additional effect of improving the relationship between Jimmy's parents. Together, the parents thought of ways in which they could buffer consequences that otherwise might traumatize Jimmy. They asked Jimmy for his input on which buffers would help him with school pressures.

The parents took the steps necessary to buffer the consequences Jimmy would encounter when he was finally in charge. They met with his teachers to explain that, with their support, Jimmy was about to take charge of his own affairs, and had the right to fail or succeed. The school, for its part, was to give Jimmy fair consequences and mark him fairly. The parents' hope was that Jimmy would not turn against education any more than he already had. They were willing to accept any change in Jimmy's school placement that their son approved of for himself, should that occur. Jimmy felt very much in charge, and very much supported. If he made a mistake, or wanted to change something in his school schedule, his parents would back him up. They wrote the excuses he needed to avoid disciplinary measures that could prove traumatic and threaten his progress. All his parents asked was that he learn from his mistakes, which happens anyway when no one assumes the punitive *make-sure* role.

The parents also made it clear that Jimmy would be responsible for treating adults with dignity and respect, no matter what the provocation otherwise. He didn't have to perform for them, but he had to represent his family favorably with good conduct. Regarding peers, he had to take responsibility for associating with those who were safe. Otherwise, the privileges would be lost. Jimmy's father feared initially that Jimmy would take advantage of his privileges. He was surprised, however, by how sensible his son turned out to be. Jimmy became even-tempered and helpful. He dropped some classes, and created for himself many more opportunities to socialize in school. He also did well in the classes he chose, and knew he could exercise his right to do poorly, as well as his privilege to do well.

A year after initially being surrounded with consequences designed to teach and strengthen him, Jimmy realized he could be successful in school. I remember his words after his first report card showed all passing grades, including a few Bs. "Now I know I can do it myself, without help . . . It wasn't that hard, either! . . . I like Bs and Cs. I don't want to do any better than that. Bs and Cs are for me, except in health. I hate that class. It deserves a D." Jimmy had no reason to lie. He had no reason to rebel. He had friends, and his parents were his friends. He was talkative, confident, and happy. In fact, Jimmy had matured in many ways.

5 The Natural-Consequences Program

Intervention 1: Consequences That Teach and Strengthen

Step 1: Preparing Consequences

Consequences will lead to growth if they meet two important conditions: (1) they are administered from a positive, business-like stance, and (2) they are intense enough to challenge, but are buffered enough to be tolerated without causing trauma. A positive, business-like attitude buffers the consequences, and avoids the provoking of retaliation. Calm delivery invites contemplation and learning. Aggressive delivery invites defensive responses, including protest and rebellion, against what is perceived to be an attack. It is only human for a parent to become angry and aggressive when delivering consequences. However, it is not smart or effective to do so.

Consequences must be reasonable to yield growth. Challenging but reasonable consequences create necessity, strengthen and teach. Unreasonably difficult consequences can prove debilitating because they traumatize. Trauma injures, weakens, and pulls for repetition of the incident. Keep consequences in that middle zone between traumatic and too easy. Think, "Challenging but tolerable."

Consequences must also be intelligently conceived. They should teach children the same lessons as those that apply in real life. They should approximate natural consequences, so that the adaptive brain acquires responses that work in real life. The central lesson I want to teach about privileges is this: *If you misuse it, you lose it. If you respect it, it grows. If you lose it, you must engage in a reparative act to get it back.* Also part of the lesson is the requirement that the reparation demanded must be reasonable. You will learn a simple procedure to determine consequences that meet these criteria.

Allowing vs. Dispensing Consequences

I will divide consequences for misused privileges into two categories: those that affect the child's life outside the family, and those that affect the family directly. The same episode can affect families in different ways. For example, missing the school bus in the morning can impact mostly his school life when the situation involves an older child who can get himself to school, or a parent with flexible work hours, who can take the child to school later. On the other hand, the same missed bus can primarily affect the family when the situation involves the parent of a young child who must get to work on time, or face losing his job.

You will allow natural consequences to occur in instances where the infractions committed primarily affect the child's life outside the home. You will dispense simulations of natural consequences in instances where the infractions primarily affect the family.

The dividing line between allow and dispense situations may not, however, be easy for some over-involved and sensitive parents to discern. They will feel that most infractions have a primary impact on themselves and their families, and, therefore, that each infraction, anywhere, is, without exception, a Hotspot requiring the parents to fashion the consequences.

I have special advice for parents experiencing this difficulty. It is that the program will not work under these conditions because the placing of every Hotspot in the dispense zone establishes the parent in a universal *make-sure*, controlling role in which natural forces outside the home play no part. To avoid this self-defeating habit, ask yourself, if you are a parent, at whom the infraction is directed. If it involves someone other than yourself, the consequence belongs in the allow zone. You permit the consequence to happen, but don't originate it. Sources of consequences outside the family can include biological (if you don't bathe, you itch), school (if you don't do your homework, you fall behind, lower your grade, or face detention), or social (you are ostracized by your friends). You dispense simulations of natural consequences when the infraction will not invite consequences from any source other than you.

Your priority as a *Natural-Consequences Parent*, in fact, is to arrange for as many consequences to fall into the allow zone as possible. This is because any Hotspot that falls into the allow zone is off your plate for good.

Allowing Consequences

Consider the metaphor of a spigot attached to a powerful fire hose when you are entering the realm of allowing consequences. You close the spigot to protect your child from life's consequences. You open it to allow full, unprotected consequences. Closing the spigot stands for buffering. Opening the spigot stands for allowing. The power in the hose represents the assumption that life's natural consequences can be very harsh. Your role in allowing is to decide how much to open the spigot. Too little will fail to teach or strengthen. Too much will traumatize and weaken. It is better to err on the side of too little. So, when in doubt, buffer.

It is generally a good idea to consult with your children before deciding how much to buffer a consequence. You have put your children in charge. They know what happened, and what's fair. It is your child's responsibility to decide whether the consequences he faces are reasonable or excessive. You can buffer consequences by writing excuses, making allowances, changing activities, or hiring professional help to protect your child. But your child must be in good standing with you to receive this level of support.

Dispensing Consequences

You enter the realm of dispensing when the infraction the child has committed has its primary impact on the family. Different degrees of privilege loss are possible. The degree of loss should correspond to the type of impact the infraction had on the family, and the type of misuse involved. The reparation involved in restoring the privilege should also correspond to the level of impact on the family, but it should be largely determined by the lesson from consequences that needs to be learned.

Different degrees of privilege loss are possible. The mildest level is the loss of a specific privilege. (1) For example, misuse a bicycle or car and the child loses use of it until he can demonstrate respect for that privilege. The same principle holds for losing kitchen and social privileges. (2) The next level is loss of the support of a parent. I call this Off Duty. This means the parent stops providing services normally offered, including rides, money, wake-up calls, other kinds of reminders, bedtime stories, and tutoring. (3) The most severe consequence you can deliver as a parent is Off Privileges, as discussed in the previous section under "Extending Time Out to Older Children." The child who has lost a specific privilege, and continues to defy and harm the family, will lose all family privileges until respect for the family has been demonstrated. Loss of privileges extends to anything electrically powered, including TV, radio, stereo, computer, video games and tele-phone, as well as anything peer-related, including having a friend over, visiting friends, and participating in sports or clubs. Loss of privileges also extends to anything that involves contact with fam-ily, including the availability of money, transportation, and play with siblings, whether or not the child has made commitments to be doing other things somewhere else.

Three levels of infraction are possible, depending on the privi-lege misused, and the number of family members it affects. Rang-ing from least to most harmful, the degrees of infraction can in-volve: (1) misusing family possessions — TV, stereo, phone, bi-cycle, tools, car, an area of the house, like kitchen or playroom; (2) abusing a family member, as in personal attacks, unreasonable resistance to parental help, refusal to help with chores, violation of personal property, teasing, and bullying; (3) misusing privileges in a way that affects the entire family, like embarrassing the family in public, making the family late for an important event, and gen-erally spoiling the family atmosphere.

The three degrees of possible privilege loss should correspond to the level of infraction committed, and take into account the fam-ily member or members affected. (1) Your child loses the privi-lege of the family possession that was misused. Misuse a car, he loses access to the car. Misuse the kitchen, he loses use of the kitchen. (2) The parent will go Off Duty should the child misuse parental help. The child will forfeit a ride, help with homework, and help with waking up or going to sleep. (3) Most other misuses of privileges will warrant the Off Privileges status, meaning loss of all family privileges, as these transgressions will most likely impact the entire family.

Coming Up with a Reparation

Loss of privileges teaches that "if you misuse it, you lose it." The reparation teaches that "if you respect it, you get it back." A reparation that teaches proper use of the misused privilege needs to accompany each loss of privilege. The child must perform reparative duties to compensate for the damage done to the family relationship, and to demonstrate learning. The reparation should be reasonable. Moreover, you should dispense your reparations in writing once you decide what they should be. This is especially important when you first implement the program.

Reparations that teach important lessons must change with each infraction. Keep two objectives in mind: (1) The reparation should offset the nature of the infraction, if possible. (2) The reparation should compensate the individual or the family for the amount of discomfort caused them.

A reparation undoes the infraction when it has the opposite effect of the original damage. It should demonstrate respectful use of the privilege lost. If the child spills milk, he cleans it up and replaces the milk. If he upsets someone, he entertains them. If he shows disrespect for someone, he finds a way of honoring them. If he embarrasses someone, he helps restore their pride. If he excludes someone from an activity, he later includes them. If he breaks something, he fixes it. If he lacks the ability or money to complete a repair, he performs some compensating work for the family, matching the cost of the item as closely as possible.

Reparations that undo infractions are positive by definition. Since the infraction was negative, undoing it entails a positive. The ideal reparation demonstrates to the child the advantages of using privileges with respect. Reparations will become monotonous and negative if they don't undo the infraction committed. Every time a child commits an infraction he will have to do cleanup work, or perform some other undesirable task. Cleanup will feel very different to a child that has made a mess than to a child who has teased a younger sibling. Creating a fun game for a tormented younger sibling will feel more constructive than cleanup work. Such a reparation will illustrate the value of being a good brother or sister. Using positive and creative reparations will influence your AD/HD child in a positive way, because they induce positive feelings, and positive feelings invite positive behavior.

The extent of compensation to the family often involves a combination of reparations — some to undo the infraction committed, others to compensate you or the family for the amount of time the family atmosphere was ruined. Say the child's fight with a sibling proved severe enough to disrupt your activities for an entire hour. Say your dinner was ruined by the fighting. A reparation to undo misuse of sibling relationships will entail playing well together for a reasonable amount of time, say the rest of that afternoon. Performance of some work for you by the child is in order, also, to compensate you for your wasted time. Taking responsibility for arranging a very pleasant dinner would compensate you for spoiling that event. Say your child misses a ride back from a social event, and you end up having to waste thirty minutes of your time to go pick your child up. A family meeting to plan social events so this doesn't happen again will undo this infraction. Some labor-saving work to compensate you for the time lost is also in order.

The extent of the reparation you require to compensate you or the family for time lost presents its own set of complications, however. Some infractions can cause severe consequences to the family. You will need to come up with some requirement for atoning through reparations that is reasonable, or you will invite deviant behavior. Use trial and error until you develop reparations of reasonable difficulty.

A good starting point for finding a reasonable reparation is the following general rule: Reparations should involve one and one-half times the inconvenience caused the family. However, the six-year-old child who commmits an infraction that might require hours of reparation cannot be expected to compensate the family to that extent. The teenager who causes $500 worth of damage to property cannot be expected to come up with $750. In these cases, the reparation becomes token. However, the child who performs on even a token level of reparation makes family more important than himself in the process. Have your child exert a reasonable effort to regain the lost privilege. This will optimize growth, and growth is the ultimate goal of parenting.

Tickets and Shuffles

The process of dispensing a *Ticket* entails writing for the child a description of the infraction committed, and the reparations needed to restore the lost privileges. The procedure is simple. It makes use of a tactic I call the *Shuffle*, which I define as walking away to escape conflict. You walk away from a Hotspot, or crisis situation, by employing the Shuffle. You then refer to the Consequences Chart you will learn how to create (**see Appendix C**), and look up the privilege loss and the reparation required for the offense involved. You write a description of the infraction, the impact it had on the family, and the reparation it will take to undo it and compensate the family for the extra burden placed upon it, if any. You hand out to the child the Ticket, much like a police officer would for a traffic violation. Finally, you remove the privileges indicated, and wait for the child to complete the reparation. You do not prompt or remind. The initiative to make good on the reparation must come from the child.

You do not give in to demands for privileges once you have dispensed a Ticket. Your child may pretend to have forgotten the infraction and approach you with requests for favors, or for restoration of the privileges lost. You ask the child to show you proof of having completed the reparation. If he does not comply, walk away.

You do not have to dispense a Ticket right away when an infraction occurs. You can let matters slide if you think the situation calls for it. You take a minute to write the Ticket, and give it to the child when it is convenient for you and your family. You may fear retaliation. You may be entertaining company. You may not feel well. There are times when it is not advisable to dispense a consequence, especially to a child who is likely to retaliate angrily. You may want to do it when your spouse, partner or friend is present. You may not want to do it until the company has left. You may not want to do it until you can get your younger children out of the way, to a friend or a neighbor's house.

Step 2: Creating a Facilitating Environment

You will launch this program in a way that establishes a foundation for building confidence by putting your children in charge of themselves, and showing them how to derive confidence from failure. Children naturally feel proud of what they do when they are in charge. They also gain strength from the weight of responsibility that comes from being in charge. You can teach children to derive confidence from failure by explaining how the greatest opportunity for self-improvement comes from recognizing and working on weaknesses.

You will formally launch the *Natural-Consequences Program* by talking with your child at different times within a couple of days. Stage these conversations at the times that suit you best.

Putting Children in Charge

Most children feel confident when they succeed, but disheartened when they fail. They will be able to learn more from their failures than from their successes, but they fear and hide their shortcomings in their efforts to obtain emotional safety. The best way to locate weaknesses is by exposing oneself to failure. Those who are ashamed of their weaknesses and seek to hide them are fated to remain stuck with them. Once your children learn to view failure as an opportunity, they will derive confidence from both winning and losing.

Hence, put your children in charge of themselves by saying something like: "I've heard that most kids reach a point where they parent themselves really well, because they come to love doing things their own way. I know you don't like me telling you what to do all the time, and I don't like it either. I want to find out if you're at one of these points in your life where you need to parent yourself. So I am going to give you a chance to show me what you can do. I know you might make some mistakes early on, but will soon become a good parent to yourself.

"I expect you to take care of your responsibilities at home, even if you are busy elsewhere. The freedom of grownups means you handle your life your own way outside of home, but take increased responsibilities at home. Adults pay rent, clean, cook and wash. Your rent payment for living here will be to help with a fair share of the housework in addition to taking care of the responsibilities in your own personal life." The amount of work you assign will vary dramatically, based on age, but the learning principle will remain the same. Younger children can contribute a token amount.

Failure as an Opportunity

Explain to your children how people who are very successful welcome failures because they have learned how to turn them into learning opportunities. They look forward to discovering weaknesses in themselves, and take pride in overcoming them. They try their very best, and then examine their weaknesses. They don't care if others see or even laugh at their exposed flaws. Those who laugh are usually hiding their own weaknesses, so they won't be improving very much. The very successful, on the other hand, know that tremendous improvement will come once they have worked on and strengthened their weak areas.

Introduce failure to your child as a valuable learning experience by saying something like: "I think you've reached a point in your life where you need to learn to invest in yourself. Many kids are afraid to fail. They avoid hard challenges because they want to hide their weaknesses, as though they were born perfect. This is a big mistake for someone who wants to become well-rounded and strong. The best way discover how you can grow the most is to look at your failures. You can grow the most and learn the most by working on weaknesses.

"Since you're still a kid, I will be glad to help you with things, but only if: (1) you can't handle things on your own, (2) you initiate the request and accept my help gladly, like you would with a good friend, and (3) you do your fair share and try your best. We can try putting you in charge of yourself this week."

Once you've had these talks, you wait for actual failures to occur. Treat these as opportunities to talk about how to find weaknesses by looking at failures; and how to turn failure into learning and strengthening. Any kid can be happy while winning with all kinds of help from Mom and Dad. The real challenge is to learn and become a better and stronger person after each failure, to learn to look at challenges as win-win situations. Either you'll win, or you'll learn.

Step 3: Escaping Hotspots

The way you escape from a conflict-laden situation can make a significant difference in how your child responds. Programs for "normal" children have established the effectiveness of counting down and then removing a privilege for non-compliance. These programs leave you susceptible to the problems of *Make-Sure Parenting*. Experience has taught that authoritative tones and angry body language pull for rebellion with AD/HD and other difficult children. There is an inherent controlling message in parental approaches like the countdown, "1-2-3 . . . That's it!" Or, "Because I said so!" This level of control wreaks of *make-sure* and is aggressive. It inspires rebellion and destroys empathy.

You can escape bouts of Control Poker by adopting a humane, reasonable stance that admits you cannot control your child, but asserts that you will not allow yourself to be taken advantage of, or mistreated in any way. You can state this firmly, confidently, and even positively. Consequences will speak for you. Consequences should teach and invite reflection, not provoke and traumatize. The fighting tone attempts to make your screaming the consequence (punishment). However, this is not an effective consequence, and will only serve to undermine the effectiveness of the consequence you designed in Step 1 of this program.

The counting down method is inherently authoritative and controlling, no matter how even-temperedly and respectfully you count. Truly difficult and AD/HD children will respond with aggression and defensiveness to any approach that conveys the message of control, "You will do as I say." Countdowns are OK with smaller children. However, older youths and teenagers will not respond well to countdowns, any more than they respond to Time Out.

Rather than counting, I recommend a message of equality and respect while you are dealing with selfishness, claims of entitlement, and rudeness — all without anger. This kind of enlightened response will not come naturally. Hence, I suggest that you learn a specific method for it. This method may be unnecessary in handling your easier child. However, with the truly challenging child it can be the factor that makes the program work.

My method for cooling Hotspots is not intended to get your child to do anything other than adopt an attitude of openness to reason, or of learning from the consequences that will follow. It is designed to convey to your child that: (1) an unfair behavior is causing problems, (2) this maladaptive behavior is having a destructive impact on you or the family, and (3) a consequence will follow. It is delivered in an emotionally honest way, but must be brief by design. Otherwise, it will appear that you want to control the outcome. The power of this intervention comes from the unspoken but implied message that you are willing to let things go, something you cannot accomplish from a *make-sure* stance. This method consists of a demand for fairness followed by a simple choice, and a few minutes upon which to reflect on this choice: cooperate or face consequences.

Join, Complain, and Walk Away

The best escape from the *make-sure* role involves a three-part response. The first part is joining. It is natural to empathize with your children's desires or complaints. The tendency of *Make-Sure Parents* is to strive to make their children happy, whatever the circumstances. If children plan an outdoor activity and it starts to rain, the *Make-Sure Parent* is expected to make the sun shine. Your natural response to difficult or impossible demands is likely to be anger. You can, however, view these situations as opportunities for growth, and let your children solve their own problems. From this wiser course of action will flow the natural ability to empathize with your children's feelings of desire, disappointment, and anger. By joining with them in their feelings, you escape conflict, and validate their experience.

The second part of your response will involve complaining. This step is critical because it exposes the ugliness of your child's behavior. A complaint does not provide your child with much of an excuse for defiant behavior. This is the opposite of what occurs with authoritative messages, which inspire retorts like: "You can't make me!"

Complaining is a natural response for most people who are being annoyed by their children's behavior. It is consistent with the consequences for disrespect dispensed in the real world, and represents an opportunity for you to teach your children that they have no right to make their own needs more important than yours. You want to deflate their self-centered, narcissistic attitude by sending the message that this stance is downright ugly. The essential message is that this is not OK. At this moment, parenting is not fun. But it is honest and non-controlling. You will convey this message succinctly, and then walk away — the third step in this natural response.

The walk-away will usually involve physically removing yourself from the conflict-laden situation. You will take a personal Time Out, during which you will not know what your child will choose to do. Your child will often surprise you with a moral choice. It is mostly in the heat of the moment created by the tit-for-tat control battles that disrespect thrives. You turn to your chart during these few minutes, and prepare to allow or dispense the appropriate consequence.

Situations involving very young children may call for detaching yourself mentally, and ignoring your children's cries while you go about your business. Children five and under may require that you join in acknowledging their feelings, while remaining quietly present to comfort them. "I know how it feels to be hungry, honey, and I know what it's like when you only want McDonald's." You don't say anything else — no explanation. You may have to repeat your joining statement several times, and offer a hug: "I know you're hungry, and I know you're upset. Come here. Give me a hug." Any hint of a solution will cause an escalation of screams and tears, like adding fuel to a fire. Wait for the tantrum to pass. As your child calms himself, he is developing valuable self-soothing abilities.

This escape move, with its joining, complaining, and walking away, is designed to forestall conflict-laden situations likely to elicit outbursts that you will end up regretting. The goal of this method is to take the energy of your presence away from your child. It also removes you from a situation in which your anger could get the better of you. Proper use of this response will result in a de-escalation of conflicts, the parents having learned to take their own Time Outs as an alternative to screaming and "losing it."

Now let's see how joining, complaining, and walking away might work for the three ways in which your children can jam your Wheel of Life:

Badgering

Some children may seek to disconcert their parents by making persistent, whiny demands and angry sounds, hoping to wear them down. This is badgering, for which a joining statement might be, "I know how much this means to you," followed by the complaint, "You're annoying me. Leave me alone!" Your body language must convey your feelings of frustration. If you're too composed, you invite attack. You are saying, in effect, "You are allowing your needs to get ugly." You should take this opportunity to teach your children that there are more important things going on in the family than their personal needs. Your final response is to walk away, which will often stop the badgering and resolve the situation.

With some oppositional-defiant children, badgering can easily escalate into verbal or physical attacks. Their assumption that a personal need gives them the right to abuse others is a reflection of immaturity and extreme feelings of entitlement. You have several choices for how to handle these attacks, should the situation go that far. I will recommend three: (1) Put on some sneakers and go for a power walk. Many of these kids are quite lazy, and will surrender after they follow you for a while. This, obviously, is not possible if you have several little children needing your supervision. (2) Dispense a consequence — if the badgering escalates to the point where it harms the family. Administer a Ticket. It may be a good idea to say something like, "If you keep this up, there will be consequences." (3) Take temporary possession, as collateral, of some item your child values highly, and then indulge him. This is by far the most effective answer to the problem of impulsivity and badgering. I suggest you use it whenever possible.

Turning Badgering Into Growth

Taking collateral is an effective response to badgering, because it resolves the situation and provides the child with a therapeutic experience for his impulsivity. It turns badgering into growth. This option works only if you can afford to indulge the child. The steps involved are simple: After you join the child's desire for indulgence, you complain about the inconveniences to you and members of the family, whose needs are equally important. Your badgering child will then offer all kinds of promises to make things right, and fulfill obligations later. "Later" is the key word. Children carried away by momentary impulses don't realize how, once they have been indulged, they will no longer have any motivation to make good on these promises. Point this out to your child. Tell him you know he will not honor his promises. Your child will swear you're wrong. This is when you take your collateral.

Explain to your child that banks have developed a system called "collateral" to resolve this very problem among adults. You are willing to give in to the present demands, as long as your child gives you some collateral — something of value to him that you will keep until you are repaid. Get this in writing. Your badgering child will agree to these terms readily. You must choose a very essential item for collateral, and specify two things in writing: (1) when repayment is due and repossession will take place, and (2) the terms for fulfilling the obligation. Let's look at an example.

"Mom, can I have five dollars to go out with my friends?"

"Oh, where are you going?" (This is the joining step of the Shuffle. The child goes on to describe what cool games his friends and he will be playing, and how wholesome this is.)

"Can I go now? Please!" (The child begs)

"I don't know. I have to think about it. I can't just think of your needs, without considering where that leaves the family. Besides, I'm busy, and I don't have five dollars. (This is the complain component of the Shuffle. Here your child will meet all of these objections with urgency and promises.)

"But I can't wait. Jimmy is coming over. And if I don't go, they'll just invite Mike, and I'll be screwed! Please! Please! Moooom!!!!" (This is getting ugly.)

"I am not going to even consider it if you attack me. Who do you think you are?" (This is your complaint — a scolding and a limit. The parent is ready to walk away, but the child continues to beg.)

"All right, Mom. I really need this!"

"Weren't you supposed to visit your Uncle Fred today and mow the lawn for us?"

"I'll do it tomorrow!"

"You'll never do it. Once you get your way, you'll blow us off. And what am I supposed to do? Fight you? No way!"

"You don't trust me!" (This is where the parent explains, and takes collateral.)

"Fine, I'll lend you the five dollars, but I have to have your skateboard as collateral. Let's write down what you will do later, and when you will do it."

"Fine. Does that mean I can go?"

"Sign here. This paper reads: 'In exchange for $5 and putting off my obligations, I agree to mow the lawn, finish my homework, and help with kitchen duties when I get back tonight (Saturday after my outing), and will have these jobs done by 2 p.m. tomorrow. I will also visit Uncle Fred tomorrow afternoon. If the work is not done at 2 p.m., I give up my skateboard until all work is done.'"

This procedure provides a remedy for a common problem that impulsive individuals present — that of seeking immediate gratification without considering later consequences. These individuals purchase things they don't really need and canët pay for. They jump mindlessly into commitments they can't fulfill. They leave assignments for the last minute. The collateral intervention gets you off the hook when your child is badgering you for those five dollars, that dinner at McDonald's, or that outing with friends. It later teaches your child a lesson. Your child will try to escape payback once he has achieved his immediate goal. Normally this would lead to another fight, the child escaping responsibility, and the cycle repeating itself without consequences to the child, and with no learning taking place. The collateral intervention reverses this. It leaves the child facing loss of a valuable asset, which threat provides the need to make good on the promises. Fulfilling the obligation under these conditions encourages a feeling of regret for impulsive indulgence. This will strengthen your child and provide a need to practice impulse control.

Dawdling

The joining statement for dawdling, or the seemingly endless prolonging or avoidance of tasks, might sound something like, "Fine, I never liked doing homework, either," and your complaint, "I don't constantly need to remind you to do your homework. If you're not going to appreciate my help, remind yourself!" You should take this opportunity to teach your child the consequential lesson that may occur if he continues to dawdle. You might say, "It's OK with me if you don't practice your piano. But this attitude will affect how you progress, and I'm not going to waste my money on your lessons! It's your choice." For different dawdling situations, you might point out how your child may be headed for trouble at school, be late for a party, or anger friends. You then walk away and let consequences happen. You might say: "Some people need to learn the hard way. Maybe you need to fail."

Dawdling situations require consequences. The question is whether to allow the world to impose consequences, or whether to dispense them yourself, and write a Ticket. Refer to your consequence and reparation chart. The goal of the Shuffle for dawdling is to escape the heat of the moment. You want to be out of the role in which you want good things more than your child does. You want your child in charge, so his adaptive brain functions are fully engaged, and growth can take place.

Personal Attacks

In the event of personal attack, you will use the joining statement, "I know you're angry." Your complaint statement will be, "Your anger does not give you the right to talk to me this way!" Or, "Why take it out on me?" And then, as a consequence, you walk away, withdrawing your support. Treat personal attacks like you would obscene phone calls. Hang up!

Your children's goals in using personal attack may include: (1) to discharge anger, (2) to get even, and (3) to upset you enough to make you "lose it." After losing it, you will feel guilty, and often you will try to make up. The need to reconcile frequently drives parents to soften, and to offer payoffs. This effectively blocks the child's growth.

In certain situations, your children will try things like making scenes in public to hold you hostage to their demands. An example statement, "But moMMMm!!!" loudly. "You never buy me candy bars. You promised!" You should view these situations as opportunities to show your children that you are willing to expose yourself to public humiliation if that's what it takes to get past the oppositional phase. After having unsuccessfully attempted this tactic, your child will feel foolish for having embarrassed you.

Finally, you should view the emotional fits that occur in these situations as clearing the way for something better. Look at tantrums as ways to stabilize your children's moods, to get past fits of entitlement, and to recover the image of children who are genuine and appreciative. Do not mistake tantrums for signs that what you're doing is wrong. Tantrums are followed by self-correction. Children need to learn self-soothing and self- control. Working out of a tantrum is an essential life-skill.

Some Examples

Consider the following situations and how you might escape them, using the steps of join, complain, and walk away. As you will see, your escape move dilutes the angry atmosphere, and creates a brief space in which to think.

1. The child says: "You're an idiot. All other parents give their kids rides anytime. You and your stupid business calls. Do'em later." The child uses attack and street talk so that the parent will become incensed and lose his composure. In the escape move, the parent joins, but complains, saying playfully: "Hey, I know the mall's fun, but you're the idiot if you can't see that business calls keep the roof over our heads."

2. The child may begin by saying, "Other parents give their kids . . ."

The escape move goes this way: "You wanna compare me to other parents who cater to their kids' every whim? How about I compare you to kids who are working on next week's paper already? Oh, but I don't want to get into that. I don't wanna get into telling you how to run your school life. Don't tell me how to run my business life (complaint). Look . . . I've got to take care of my business. Maybe you can make family first in your life and still manage to have some fun (challenge)."

3. The child says: "I'm not following these rules. You're an asshole!" The word "asshole" is used to provoke parents into losing it. The escape move is as follows: "I hate a lot of rules, too (joining). But you're an asshole if you can't put the family first (again, complaint, said in a playful tone). I don't have time for this stuff (walk away)."

4. Father is about to rig a sailboat for the first time of the season. Son and son's girlfriend stand around watching. Much to the father's surprise, the son shows great interest and enthusiasm.

He wants to rig the boat himself, and take his girlfriend out on the first sail of the season. Father has done most of the prep work on the boat, and feels it is his right to rig it and take it out. The son pushes and pushes for dad to let him rig the boat, and be the first to sail. He obviously wants to impress his girlfriend. Father's frustration mounts as he senses the manipulation. He finally says very firmly, but in a childish tone: "NO! It's my toy, and I'll play with it when I want to." This ends the discussion. (The father Shuffled by acting more childlike than his son, thus reversing the magnetic polarities of the relationship and ending the struggle.)

5. A high school student's friend, who drives him to school, is ill. Father, who must now drive his son to school, is worried that the son will regress to previous habits, and will struggle in the morning about getting up for school. The father reverses the magnetic polarities of the relationship by putting his son in charge of making sure he gets up in time to take him to school. The next morning the father wakes up on time, but stays in bed until his son reprimands him for being late, and tells the father to get moving, or he'll be late.

6. A child dawdles when he's supposed to be working on a major research project. The child clearly isn't producing, and a report is due. School work primarily affects the child's life outside of home. Accordingly, the project falls into the allow zone. The parents feel that it is essential to issue a reminder as a buffer, but don't want to go any further, make a Hotspot out of the situation, and risk giving the child an excuse for not completing the assignment.

One of the parents says: "I know getting started on research is a pain. When I had to do it, I found it really hard, too (joining). You're not being fair to yourself by not even getting your books out, though. (complaint). Some people seem to have to learn the hard way. Maybe that's you. Failure is a very good teacher (challenge)." This kind of challenge reverses the magnetic polarities of the *make-sure parent* who has been protecting the unmotivated child.

7. A child is not cleaning up the family room, which is on his list of jobs to do for the family. The parent says: "Look, I hate bending over and picking things up, too. Especially when it's just gonna get messy again soon, anyway (joining). But it's on your list for contributing to the family, and it won't be fair if you ask us to do things for you when you haven't done your part (complaint). Make your own decision, but make it fair, or you'll be on your own (without family privileges) when all the good shows are on, and your friends are around (challenge)."

Dispensing Consequences

Now you will use the Consequences Chart to dispense consequences for the most common Hotspots in your home. Each time you encounter a Hotspot, you will: (1) escape from it, (2) refer to your personal consequences chart, (3) write up the Ticket, and (4) cut the privileges involved. Follow this procedure any time you encounter a routine Hotspot.

Keep in mind the following suggestions when dispensing Tickets:

1. Generally, do not remove privileges immediately, unless this is part of going Off-Duty. It is better to Shuffle out of the situation, and challenge the child to make it fair for the family. This avoids a tit-for-tat atmosphere, and prevents retaliation. Jack kicked his mother, Sarah, when she didn't cater to one of his demands. She immediately took his baseball equipment for his "rudeness." He retaliated by saying she had been rude by taking his baseball equipment, and proceeded to take the equipment back from her by force, threatening to use it, anyway. Allowing the child time to correct the situation after you Shuffle invites the child's inner parent to reflect upon the situation, and provides an opportunity to prevent

the privilege loss. Write the Ticket and wait a bit. Remove privileges and dispense the Ticket once it feels safe, and you see evidence that it is necessary to do so.

2. When you are dispensing consequences, do not specify the amount of time to be spent without privileges. Say the privileges are removed "until you have demonstrated solid evidence of fairness and respect, and shown me that you realize family needs come first."

3. When you are ticketing, try having kids write explanations of how other family members were affected by their disruptive actions, the feelings people had, and alternative strategies the child could have used to accomplish his ends without causing a disturbance. This can serve as the demonstration of respect for the misused privileges. This kind of reparation can be very helpful for some children who cannot predict other people's reactions well, are not good at stepping back and thinking of alternative strategies, or lack social skills.

Try implementing the consequences you designed, and rate their effectiveness. If a particular consequence proves ineffective, design a new consequence worksheet. Take the worksheet to your counselor or support group for input, if needed. Continue to test, adjust, and refine the different consequences you prepare until you have effective consequences for each routine Hotspot you encounter.

Seek professional help, however, for any Hotspot that doesn't respond to any of the consequences you try. There are probably obstacles to growth lurking behind Hotspots that remain problems. Such areas may need professional evaluation and treatment.

The completion of this exercise represents a major step. You are now prepared to escape Hotspots from the position of a *Make-Sure Parent*, shift to a *Natural-Consequences* stance, and administer effective consequences for oppositional-defiant behavior. Your next step will be to use family to teach social skills. You will learn to dispense consequences that will encourage contribution to the family, including chores, child-care, and help with special projects. Greater contribution to the family will teach your children respect, by having them learn to make the needs of the larger group more important than their own.

You will need some preparation before proceeding. You will need to continue to work with routine Hotspots as recommended thus far, with escape moves and Tickets, for at least three weeks. If the program is not working, however, you may need to overcome some obstacles before it will. The next section will help you troubleshoot any major problems you encounter. You may skip this intervention if the program is working well for you, and turn to "Intervention 3: Using Family to Teach Social Skills", beginning on page 100.

Intervention 2: What if I Fail?

The overwhelming majority of parents respond with great optimism when first exposed to the program, but for some the enthusiasm will fade. As training progresses, there is a predictable number of dropouts. A few continue, but seem to sink deeper into quiet disappointment as others report making breakthroughs. Experience has shown that about one-third of the parents I train struggle with the implementation of the program. I study the special needs of these cases whenever possible, and have learned a good deal. Many of the problems these parents encounter turn out to be easy to resolve. Others are predictable, but difficult to deal with. Some seem impossible.

The following sections address the most common obstacles to proper implementation of the program. They list the most common problems parents are likely to encounter, and present two interventions that are likely to help. The first two sections will help you identify obstacles you may face, and suggest some common-sense solutions. The two interventions that follow address excessive childhood rebellion, and parental inability to let go. These interventions have worked well for the majority of parents who have tried them, but the problems involved may require consultation with a professional.

What If the Scene Turns Ugly?

If you suddenly find yourself involved in an unexpected ugly scenario, you will have some work ahead of you. Your problem is very common among parents of AD/HD children. For help, you can skip ahead a few paragraphs to "Resolving Obstacle 1, Inordinate Oppositional-Defiance." This intervention addresses the challenge of the most difficult children, and the perils of adolescence. It is a more potent version of the program described above. For now, back off from whatever you have been doing, give yourself time to prepare to intervene more effectively, and arrange to have professional backing. Return to your consequences chart and your Shuffle to cope with routine Hotspots once you resume normal life.

What If I Still Can't Implement the Program?

In addition to the inordinately oppositional-defiant child, three common conditions tend to keep parents from successfully implementing this program. In order of severity, from mildest to most severe, they include: (1) parents who cannot let go of their *Make-Sure Parenting* stance, and therefore cannot put their children in charge and allow consequences; (2) parents with partners who refuse to cooperate, and undermine everything the other parent does, and (3) parents who find themselves incapable of mobilizing resources in the face of their children's resistance and demands. These three conditions will require special help.

Perhaps your child can respond reasonably well to the program, but you cannot let go of the *Make-Sure Parenting* role. If so, you probably suffer from parental neurosis. This is a condition that results when you have been attached to your child as a *Make-Sure Parent* for too long. Turn to "Resolving Obstacle 2, Parental Neurosis" in the next section if this describes your situation. Your condition is understandable, and your problem is most likely solvable.

You may live with a partner who undermines your efforts, and refuses to cooperate with, or even look at, what you're doing. Your partner may be extremely lenient, and undermine your attempts to allow or dispense consequences. Or he may be exceedingly controlling, and stuck hopelessly in the *Make-Sure Parenting* role. In either case, I suggest that you implement this program independently, as a single parent would, anytime you are alone and in charge. Allow your partner to handle the kids in his own way the rest of the time, as well as deal with consequences. It is important that you do not get involved, as this would only make you an enabler, and help extend the duration of the problem. You should walk away from parenting anytime your partner interferes with your handling of the children. You go Off Duty immediately, to use the language of natural consequences. Your partner has lost the privilege of having you as a co-parent, and must demonstrate respect for this privilege (perform reparation) before getting it back.

In effect, by going Off Duty as a co-parent, you are dropping your *make-sure* role vis-a-vis your partner, and inviting him to face the limitations of his approach to parenting. Your children will burden your lenient partner with increasing demands for rescue, or they will exploit your partner's *Make-Sure Parenting* tendencies. Experience has established the increasing effectiveness of this strategy towards uncooperative partners in several cases, though it takes time. If your partner seems incompetent and begins to abuse your children, report this to the authorities, and seek professional help. As always, you must buffer the consequences to your children and your partner.

You may find yourself overwhelmed or immobilized when facing your children's resistance and demands, and unable to follow through with consequences. Your life may be chaotic. You may be plagued with problems that render you incapable of adopting a reasonable perspective, including social and economic hardships, isolation, or illness. Mental disorders are common in parents of difficult children, and these can also keep you from following through with consequences. These disorders can result from a history of family dysfunction, trauma, personal loss, hardship, disabling addictions, or biochemical imbalances that cause depression symptoms. You should seek professional help if you fall into this third category of problems.

Resolving Obstacle 1: Oppositional-Defiance

Oppositional-defiance can become extremely troublesome, persistent, and toxic in families. Children who respond to loss of privileges with undue rebellion will require a special intervention to facilitate a constructive response to the program described in this book. Strategic Therapy offers the best possible system of knowledge for this purpose. Strategic interventions rely on reverse psychology and paradox to resolve symptoms. Since oppositional states are negative, they worsen with direct pressure, but lessen with reverse psychology.

The father of Strategic Therapy was Milton Erickson, a legend in the field of psychiatry and hypnotherapy, a man truly ahead of his time. Dr. Erickson was known for resolving in moments symptoms that years of therapy had hardly touched. He developed the ability to remedy symptoms routinely, and with incredible ease.

Jay Haley studied under Dr. Erickson, and eventually organized what he had learned into a body of knowledge that became Strategic Therapy. Strategic therapists use methods like paradox and counter-paradox to achieve sudden and dramatic changes in the most deeply entrenched irrational behaviors.

Strategic methods suffer from the same black box limitations as behavioral programs. They focus on eliminating specific symptoms, but not much else. They can be used to change behaviors in any direction. They make no value judgments on whether behaviors other than the symptom should be encouraged or discouraged; whether they might be healthy or unhealthy.

This program supplements strategic intervention for oppositional-defiance with methods designed to foster the development of a healthy conscience. One way to do this is by prescribing reparative activities. Children who have made positive contributions to their families will feel better about themselves and an increased sense of belonging, will value their families more, and will more easily grasp the difference between right and wrong. Good feelings invite good behavior. It is hard to feel empathy for someone you have behaved immorally against. If you have shown disrespect for and hurt others, but have subsequently honored and supported them, you will feel more connected and welcomed in that person's life than if you had simply been punished for your infractions.

We need to establish a direction for the changes we seek to make with our strategic intervention. We want to foster the development of a conscience. To do so, we need to understand how children outgrow their inherent self-centeredness and develop a genuine ability for concern. This requires an understanding of that quality in human beings called narcissism. An understanding of the psychology of reparations and narcissism provides us with an answer to the self-centered tendencies that underlie oppositional-defiance. The strategic intervention will take care of the rest.

The Origins of Narcissism

All babies begin life in the position of royalty, with us parents as their faithful servants. Think about it. They cry, we drop whatever we're doing and run to satisfy them. Do they need a change of clothes, milk, food, nurturing, sleep, or entertainment? Whatever it is, we quickly figure it out, and take care of it, no questions asked. This state is referred to as healthy narcissism.

Narcissism in older children and adults implies an inflated ego, excessive self-importance, and disregard for the needs of others. The ability to make others feel important is all but lost, and often this obstructs the development of relationships.

Narcissism is a normal state of development, but it must be corrected with narcissistic injury, or it can become pathological. Delivering a narcissistic injury is bursting the bubble of an overly inflated ego. This process first occurs around the time of the Terrible Twos. Parents are ready to let go of their servant roles, and their children's first step is rapidly losing charm. The parents expect more. If they are busy with other matters, they want their children to wait for their needs to be attended to. They expect their children to take more responsibility for managing their own affairs.

Narcissistic injury invariably leads to what clinicians call narcissistic rage, a state, however, that invariably quickly passes. At age two, the baby responds with tantrums, the two-year-old equivalent of murderous rage. Young children feel entitled to hurt us, but are too small to pose any real threat. Common wisdom tells us to put raging children in Time Out until the fit passes. After a few minutes, there is a complete change of mood.

Once narcissistic rage passes, the deflation of the excessive ego leads to a reduction of expectations. Thereafter, children are satisfied more easily and more frequently, and end up happier, prouder, and more appreciative. This is how you foster moral development. Deflate narcissism to build self-esteem.

There is a culture, however, that encourages narcissism and offers belonging and success to attention-deficit and oppositional-defiant disorder children who have been robbed of these advantages at home and in school. This is the culture of the street gangs and clubs, which   cater to the needs of the morally immature, narcissistic child. The philosophy of this culture is one of excessive indulgence. Understanding the way of this culture will prepare you to counter its irrational logic.

The Problem of Excessive Indulgence

Narcissistic logic is that if playing for a while is fun, or if watching TV is fun, then the more we do it, the better life becomes. But this is dead wrong. The more we indulge in something, the more our brains develop a tolerance for it, and the less pleasure we derive from each subsequent indulgence. Excessive gratification, in fact, quickly yields diminishing returns, and leaves us in a trap. Once the newness wears off, we end up needing the item or activity constantly, just to feel the same happiness we felt before we ever had it. Once we lose it, we feel depressed. This is the basis of drug addiction. With this in mind, we can see the wisdom of balance, moderation and mastery. If we learn to appreciate music at lower volumes, drink alcohol in smaller amounts, or watch only an occasional TV show, our capacity for happiness is greater.

The key to a philosophy of moderation, balance and mastery is to have a large pool of challenging and productive activities to choose from, and to balance these with the kinds of indulgences we have come to depend upon. That is, we need to strike a balance between the satisfaction that comes with suffering through and mastering difficult challenges, and the pleasures resulting from indulging in TV, ice cream, candy, beer and cigarettes.

Parents, Children and Drugs

An effective way for parents to counter the problem of drugs is to focus on increasing discipline and reducing laziness, because these are areas they can control, and because drug problems become most severe in lazy children who are underachieving. Parents spend far too much time trying to catch their children in acts of deception, and then punishing them and removing their privileges. However, unless the children become stronger, and develop more discipline, these punishments and humiliating violations of privacy will also provide a strong incentive for them to improve their ability to deceive.

Yes, you might keep your child looking good during those formative years by uncovering and defeating his deceptions. With hard work, you may be able to get your uncooperative child to conform and accept just enough help from you to let you make him appear successful, with passing grades in school and a good reputation in the community. But until you deflate narcissism and strengthen your child, you have achieved very little to improve the long-term picture.

Think about it. If you were to send your narcissistically-dominated child to Harvard, or any other prestigious college or university, what do you think you would get for your money? A lazy, manipulative child. You would be much better served by making sure your child is evolving, growing stronger and investing in family, in work and in self-development. You can invest the time you have spent acting like a CIA agent into enforcing the exercise of will, which will promote honesty. Accomplishing this would allow you to give your child the freedom and privacy he needs, without worrying about whether he is using drugs or is involved in other self-destructive behavior. A child who is strong and successful will do a lot less damage in hard-earned free time than a child who has been allowed to become lazy, demanding, self centered and bored, and who has lots of time to kill.

Methods made available through programs like Drug Abuse Resistance Education (DARE) are warranted when drug use impedes your child's development. Contact your local police department for programs in your area. Rest assured, they will not prosecute your child without your consent.

The Consequences of a Deviant Attachment

We have already established that Attachment Theory can prepare you to face many of the irrational behaviors you will encounter. It can explain the driving force behind much of your narcissistically-dominated child's behavior.

Starting early in life, our growth is literally determined by the nature of our attachments. A healthy attachment humanizes and promotes basic abilities that allow us to evolve in a healthy direction, possessed of qualities including trust, the ability to empathize, to feel concern for others, for self-soothing, a sense of security, self-esteem, and a conscience. An anxious, neglectful or traumatic attachment promotes distrust, callousness, insensitivity, insecurity, anxiety, depression, aggression, shame, and immorality. Youths that are traumatized early in life often fail to develop empathy or a conscience, and thus their socialization process is crippled, sometimes for life.

The term corrective relationship is used to describe an attachment that can withstand the deviant behaviors that stem from earlier traumatic experiences, that can reverse these deviant attachment patterns, and that can forge a new bond that will fundamentally change the course of that individual's development.

Attachment Theory presents us with grave concerns, but also gives us great hope. Youths emulate the behaviors of those to whom they are attached. Hence, by forming a strong bond with a child, we can mold and largely determine his fundamental attitude toward the world. When a child attaches in a healthy way, he is capable of a complete transformation in a positive direction, all in a very short period of time. Children remain malleable and open to such sweeping changes. Similarly, when a child attaches in a deviant way, we see a fast and profound transformation in a destructive direction.

An unhealthy and traumatic attachment later in life can undermine much of the development that has been achieved through earlier attachments. This is the tragedy behind trauma. It is in the nature of the attachment system to repeat the trauma, and it does so with intensity. Hence, you can imbue your troubled child with deep love and devotion, and, later on in life, an authority figure can, through coercion, undo a significant portion of your work by forming and maintaining an unhealthy attachment with your child. This later bond can arrest the developmental process.

Traumatic attachments to coercive teachers can dramatically alter an AD/HD child's view of authority — from seeing these teachers as desirable role models to seeing them as oppressors. Should parents attempt to enforce discipline in such individuals, the traumatic attachment will spread from school to home. This will undermine your earlier trusting bond, leaving your child with a rebellious attitude towards authority, and an openness toward anti-social influences.

The next section will discuss the only way to save your children from the consequences of a deviant attachment forged by unreasonable authority, or by the deviance of the streets.

Resolving Narcissism Through Hook Items

This intervention introduces the term *Hook Items* to describe the few specific privileges that have a spellbinding impact on narcissistically-entitled children. The different terminology is called for to address the unique and addictive quality of these privileges on these children. These are the only privileges that influence these children. They are all that these children seem to care about when they are in their narcissistic and defiant states. Hook Items quickly become obsessions, and easily become the basis for deviant behaviors. These children seem ready to sell their souls to gain access to them.

Hook Items involve specific privileges that are usually related to the peer world, either electronic, including TV, stereo, phone, and video games, or flesh and blood, including having friends over, sleep-over dates, and involvement in clubs and sports. Drugs and alcohol represent the ultimate in Hook Items.

V. R. Sherwood (1990) proposed a method for getting past the narcissistic resistances of rebellious ADD youths. He identified this resistance as the key obstacle to helping these children accept aid. He established the importance of overcoming narcissistic resistances as the first stage of treatment for conduct disorders.

Sherwood recommended a three-step process to counter narcissistic resistances. First, join the child in his grandiose self-importance, anti-authority attitude. This translates into joining your child in his feelings toward activities, as in the Shuffle joining statement. Second, deliver a reasonable but significant blow to his ego (a narcissistic injury). This deflates the child, but earns his respect and encourages him to take a more realistic view of the relationship. And third, praise the child for having risen to the challenge in a realistic, productive and respectful manner.

You want the consequences of narcissistic injury to resemble closely what occurs in the natural peer world for misusing a relationship. The leader of a clique has the power to cut children off from their peers. You want to command this kind of respect. You become the once-popular take-charge TV character, "the Fonz." At the first sign of disrespect, you snap your fingers and, poof, the peer world is gone, both electronic and flesh and blood. The enforcement of fair consequences will not harm your child. Once you have adopted this position of respect, your child will never see you with the same eyes again.

Consequences for Deflating Narcissism

A conduct-disordered child will seem like a formidable opponent to any adult that tries to enforce the discipline of conformity. Recall from our previous segment that the conduct-disordered child seeks to borrow the frontal lobes of others to avoid work, while, at the same time, becoming a consummate fighter against authority figures, and an expert player of peer-world games. He has developed a talent for fighting and for indulging in excessive play that makes him a deadly adversary. The conduct-disordered child feels perfectly comfortable in a vicious battle with the school principal, or even a police officer, after having cut school to spend the day at the local pool hall.

However, the conduct-disordered child has one obvious weak spot which becomes evident in the light of our new understanding of the addictive property of Hook Items. The narcissistically-entitled child is extremely vulnerable to having his hitherto constant supply of Hook Items cut off. As long as you cut off access to Hook Items and to the peer world; and as long as you avoid fighting you will be able to counter narcissistic resistance. The effect is like Kryptonite on Superman. The nervous system that has become dependent on a constant flow of Hook Items to provide satisfaction will quickly crash. The child will fall into a depressive state for the moment.

When you first cut off Hook Items, the ensuing crash will lead to a major tantrum, and an attempt to lure you into war. However, once you counter by creating distance the tantrum will run its course and fade, and the child will reach a healthy state of depression. This dysphoric state is healthy because it results from puncturing the child's massively over-inflated ego. Once the child has had to endure this depressive position, the brain will reset to normal its responsiveness to indulgence.

There is no fair and constant system that can contain the narcissistically-entitled child. This is because the child uses the across-the-board character of rules as a way to spoil things for the family. Consider what you believe to be the equitable division of obligations and responsibilities in your family, which will be described later in this book as the *Fairness Contract* (**Appendix B**). For violations, you cut off access to the peer world. You hand out lists. Then, the child figures it out that no one gets to watch TV until he has completed his work, supposedly in a spirit of collaboration and fairness. If TV is denied to him, it is denied to everyone. He will ask, "So if I don't finish all of my work, sister doesn't get to watch TV? Is that right?" The child then refuses to work, and gladly does without Hook Items, meanwhile deriving his excitement from seeing sister suffer, and wondering exactly when the situation will cause you to lose your poise. Thus, the child proceeds to make the loss-of-privileges program inconvenient for the family as a whole, and fights to have the family declare the program a failure.

Consider the example of dispensing consequences for routine Hotspots. The child agrees to all contingencies, starts to act out; then waits for you to need family cooperation to get to church on time. Sensing your need, the child strikes without mercy. He refuses to cooperate, fights the Time Out, and holds you hostage: "If I get dressed, will you take me to the mall afterwards?"

Your answer to your child's attempts to spoil the program is to be strategically inconsistent. You'll be consistent only to the extent of making sure these manipulations don't pay off. You change the rules so that sister can still watch TV when brother hasn't done his chores. You promise the child the world, effective after church, and change your mind later. In short, you do whatever it takes — honest or dishonest, consistent or inconsistent — to avoid delivering the payoff your child expects his manipulations will produce. You maintain the integrity of the program.

Once more, you will use the same psychology of allowing and dispensing privileges that we introduced in Chapter 4, under "Extending Time Out to Older Children," and which you have used to design and deliver all consequences in Intervention 1. The child who has misused the privilege of being part of the family loses it. The infraction usually impacts directly on you or your family. Hence, you enter the dispense realm. The consequence is Off Privileges. You will Shuffle out of any request for privileges until reparation has been completed. The major differences that make this application unique include: (1) a much trickier way of removing the privileges; (2) an emphasis on losing the Hook Item, with much less emphasis on other privileges, since they don't matter; and (3) the reparation will be especially difficult. This is a principle derived from Strategic Theory, based on the work of Jay Haley, who developed a specific intervention for extreme symptoms. He called it Ordeal Therapy.

Narcissistic Deflation
Step 1: Write the Ticket

Operate according to this slogan: "Don't fight, write." It works. When the narcissistic child invites trouble, rather than fight you walk away quietly, and start writing a Ticket. You deliver your

Shuffle (join, complain and walk away), and mention briefly the necessity of having to write up a complaint. If the child continues to indulge and argue, you get tricky. Act as though you're giving up, and allow him to indulge. You don't want any confrontation, because that's excitement. You want calm, so you can think clearly when you write.

You take your time as you write, and inject some playfulness into the process. You seek an inspired consequence for the child's latest ploy. The consequence is always a state of Off Privileges (**see Consequences for Routine Hotspots, Appendix C**). The reparation is something constructive that will re-establish respect for you, and fairness for the family.

The reparation should always include: (1) extra chores to compensate for wasted time,   (2) a day of humble behavior, during which your child's needs are made less important than those of the rest of the family, and (3) proof of having learned from the experience. I will call the day of humble behavior Humble Status, meaning that your child must consider people more important than objects and activities. The humble one simply wants to be with the family, no matter what the family does. Finally, the child is required to do some research that demonstrates learning from the experience, the opposite of blaming everyone else and being defensive. Your child can present at the dinner table an understanding of what happened that shows he understood what he did wrong, and that he knows how he will handle it differently next time. No rushing through it, because this would imply that the process is not important.

In any case, with your Ticket all written up and copies made, remove yourself and all family privileges, leaving no Hook Items behind.

Step 2: Administer the Ticket

Remember to deliver the Ticket at your convenience, not the child's. Perhaps you pretended the child had gotten away with things yesterday, and removed all privileges after he went off to school today. The Ticket awaits him after school. The element of surprise is on your side.

Step 3: Watch With Detachment

When you remove privileges there is normally an initial period of eruption that precedes the extinction of a behavior. Expect an attack. Remember that the storm is relatively short, the calm that follows relatively long. The eruptions become shorter, and the calms longer and longer until the maladaptive behavior vanishes. When attacked, don't say anything. Remain devoid of emotion, poker-faced, businesslike, and distant. The child's disruptive side will be off balance because it expected you to become frantic, controlling, intense. You will see maneuvers to charm, manipulate, deceive, explode or quietly cause harm. Then will follow the longest campaign of revenge the child can muster. If you're not there as an audience, your child may decide to save face and get on with the fulfillment of the reparations.

Step 4: Eliminate Hook Items

The key from this point on is to pile up enough reparations to keep the child starved for excitement and Hook Items for days, weeks if necessary. The three steps of the reparation — (1) work detail (while Off Privileges), (2) humble status (with conditional privileges), and (3) the final exam (which restores full privileges) — require a graduation to move on to the next step. Failure at each step means going back to the previous one. For example, a humble one who has been destructive goes back to work duty. A failure means going back to Humble Status.

Once you administer the Ticket, you hand your child the complaint with the list of reparations involved, and he discovers all Hook Items cut off, and extra chores to be done. This is like Off Privileges, and it lasts indefinitely, until all the work is done. Work detail often brings out the best in your child, because his self-centered attitude has been deflated. Your child's brain chemistry has had a chance to normalize.

Once the chores are complete, your child graduates to Humble Status. Here your child has to consider other people more important than himself. Now he has access to Hook Items, but only where, when, and how other family members want them used. Your child goes from no Hook Items and work duty to regaining partial privileges, as long as he can make others feel important. You should be a kind host to your child in Humble Status. You plan activities that are potentially enjoyable for everyone. You are patient as you watch your child gradually become demanding, placing his or her needs before those of others. This is to be expected with an AD/HD child. You remind him of his status by saying: "Didn't you want this to count as a humble day? Aren't you supposed to say, 'Whatever we do is fine with me as long as we are together?' You're not supposed to demand anything. Remember?"

After a day of work detail without privileges, and a day or two on Humble Status, your child is ready for the final exam. If the child doesn't want to talk, or doesn't have good answers, that's fine. He can remain humble another day and try again tomorrow. Of course, you should keep your approach reasonable. Don't expect a level of moral development that is not there.

It's hard to put your child through such an ordeal. You only want to operate at this level if all the exercises described above fail to alter your child's attitude. You can find consolation in knowing that eventually your child will come back happy, trustworthy, well-adjusted, and without a trace of resentment for what has happened. Think of it as though you are removing a parasite from your child's neck. You will be left with a happier child, and a healthier family.

Step 5: Empower Your Child

Once the reparations have been fulfilled, it's time to empower your child, time to give him a sense of authority by encouraging his access to the peer world. Restore a state of full privileges. However, expect your child to continue to contribute to the family, and fulfill all responsibilities according to a list of priorities that we will call the Order of Importance (**see Appendix A**).

You need to avoid a typical mistake that parents make when they take freedom from one extreme to the other. Some parents avoid the extreme of grounding their children by extending only minimal privileges until their misbehavior has reached intolerable proportions. Then, once the children return to their best behavior, the parents go overboard in providing Hook Items, or they become lenient in their demands. They return to doing things for the children, making sure they are happy and successful. Initially, the good behavior will continue with this catering. However, the manipulative, narcissistic tactics will gradually return, along with extreme misbehavior.

Each time you go through the process of Ticketing to remove Hook Items, the child's tactics become less extreme. The reparations are completed more easily, and the ensuing happiness will last longer. The end result will be a well adjusted child who has mastered narcissism.

Resolving Obstacle 2: Parental Neurosis

Parental neurosis develops when, in the face of oppositional behaviors, parents mandate goodness and punish their children's failure-bound behaviors. The children dread and avoid situations that represent obstacles to growth. Make-sure parents respond with excessive efforts to counter their children's regressive tendencies. They try to make up for their children's deficient efforts, and incessantly push them toward success. In return for their efforts, these parents encounter a draining impact from their children's resistance. Parents understandably worry and double their efforts to control and supplement. Yet, their efforts yield them nothing but poorer performance, more resistance, and more drain. It is only a question of time before this unnatural cycle will cause a form of neurosis in the parents, and ODD in the children.

Society routinely prescribes *Make-Sure Parenting*, as though one approach to child-rearing could prove effective with all kinds of children. *Make-Sure Parenting*, however, will only work with certain temperaments. Prescribing a uniform approach to parenting creates serious problems for families with AD/HD and other problem children. In order to maintain a positive image in society, these parents will deny the problems they experience. They sacrifice chances of growth in order to keep the ugly secret of their family Wheel of Life being jammed regularly, for hours at a time. We don't hear from them that it took three hours of hell and abuse to get the family dressed and smiling so nicely for church. This secret will grow increasingly burdensome until it becomes a full-blown parental neurosis.

We see continual episodes of extreme and irrational outbursts when parental neurosis is fully developed. This is referred to as "losing it." Parental tantrums give oppositional children a message of victory. These children turn to self pity and tears, and pull for a nurturance that has been lacking because of their spoiling tactics. They know that remorse, reconciliation, and leniency will follow. They feel a vicarious discharge of their negative energy, and they feel justified in defying parental authority.

The Cause of Parental Neurosis

Don't take offense at the term "parental neurosis." This condition is the natural result of trying to enforce *Make-Sure Parenting* for a prolongued period with an AD/HD or difficult child. Neurosis is an old-fashioned name for an anxiety disorder, which is really a combination of excessive worry and irrational thought. One feeds the other. The irrational thinking provides greater cause for worry, and worry invites further irrational thinking, and ineffective solutions. The term neuroticism has been used to refer to the irrational thinking process involved in anxiety disorders.

Neuroticism occurs around issues of control. The less realistic or adaptive the attempts to control, the more likely they are to cause neuroticism. Classic examples include ritualistic behavior, superstition, or magical thinking. Less adaptive behaviors will provide short-term relief, but do little to resolve the problem. Hence, the problem returns. The person responds to the inevitable resurgence of the problem with increased worry, and an intensification of the unrealistic solution. The cycle goes on. Extreme cases of neuroticism reach absurd levels, as in individuals who wash their hands hundreds of times a day to prevent catastrophic events from befalling their loved ones, or who control food and weight until their relationships succeed, they find great career opportunities, or they are finally appreciated by insensitive relatives.

Those who are in close contact with impulsive or compulsive individuals are very likely to develop neuroticism. Attempting to control individuals who refuse to be controlled, and are unable to control themselves, is a leading cause of neurosis. It is among the most common ways to end up in futile and irrational control battles with forces that are beyond control. Such a scenario is nothing to be ashamed of. It certainly doesn't mean you are a neurotic person. Look at those who are closely connected to gamblers, drinkers, drug addicts, control freaks, and workaholics. They are called enablers. They tend to play a critical role in allowing individuals who are out of control to maintain lives of indulgence.

Enablers tend to keep secret the troubling behaviors of those on whom they depend. They feel a need to protect the impulsive individuals they enable. They also strive to protect their families by presenting a positive image for all to see. They tend to struggle to keep those whom they enable from losing control. They may, for example, struggle to stop gamblers from taking trips to Atlantic City and its casinos, change the lifestyle of those with irrational eating patterns, or prevent alcoholics from drinking. Enablers become so wrapped up with those they strive to control that they neglect their personal lives.

Impulsive individuals sense their enablers' need to keep them under control, and take advantage of it: "If you don't cater to me, I may have no choice but to go on a gambling feast!" "So let me watch this show," "Let me have this money," "Do this for me."

There is no reason why parents responsible for the behavior of AD/HD children should differ in any way from those who deal with other impulsive disorders, including gambling and drinking to excess. AD/HD individuals suffer from impulsive behaviors that are nearly impossible to control, just as do alcoholics and drug or gambling addicts. Attempting to make sure AD/HD children do everything they are supposed to is an effort as futile as getting an alcoholic to stop drinking, or an eating-disorder sufferer to eat normally. This is doubly true when you try to make the AD/HD individual fulfill the requirements of an environment to which he is not suited.

The answer to neurotic thinking is to reduce the fear and increase the adaptability of the attempt to control the situation. You will need to understand this process before you become free to challenge it. The adaptive solutions to your AD/HD child will follow.

Recognizing Parental Neurosis

You can recognize parental neurosis by your persistent but unspoken worry that your children will fail if they are allowed to take charge of their own affairs.   Parents in this state of mind assume that children's experiences of failure will trigger a persistent and escalating pattern of discouragement — a downward spiral into despair. Once this spiral is set in motion, the parents unconsciously anticipate an uninterrupted continuation of the downward trajectory, with disaster ahead for their children, and nothing to stop it. These parents assume their children have no internal drive to succeed, no ability to overcome adversity on their own. The truth is, however, that the situation they worry about and struggle to avoid, which is putting their children in charge, is precisely the one that will save their children.

This fear is kept secret, but comes out indirectly in the parents' attempts to praise and support. Pressure to reveal secrets that are either pleasant or traumatic has a way of growing within us. Once something is experienced strongly, and is not talked about, it must come out one way or another. Without realizing they do so, some people behave according to patterns they keep secret.   This explains how people who have been abused end up abusing others, or become victims repeatedly of those with similar patterns.

The secret of parents who lack faith in their children's abilities is thoroughly revealed, but through nonverbal channels — with visible signs of parental worry and concern, and the desire to protect. The process takes place unconsciously. Parents don't realize they are communicating lack of faith, and children don't realize they are responding destructively to this unspoken message. Every time the parents ask, "Did you do your homework?" the kids unconsciously respond to, "Do you have a brain?" Every time the parents say, "You were wonderful," the kids hear it as, "See, if you make an effort like this every time, you can be successful just like the other kids."

The children come to respond aggressively to their parents' hidden fear of their incompetence. This lack of faith creates a tremendous distance between parents and children. We see parents praising and trying to help, and children snapping at them in response. We see kids that do not want to be seen in public with their parents. These children are simply afraid that others will witness their parents' lack of confidence in them. Yet, no one seems to know why this is happening. No one suspects that *Make-Sure Parenting* can have such an effect.

The Cure for Parental Neurosis

Parents must realize how their children's negativity and selfishness are signs they have outgrown their usefulness as their children's protectors. Children need to develop their own motivations, and to determine their own reasons for wanting to succeed. They need to outgrow their oppositional phase, and take responsibility for their own development. Parents need to let go, to give up control and trust that nature will assert itself. Parents who have come to live vicariously through their children's accomplishments will need to accept the reality of how the children actually turn out, and perhaps mourn the difference between that and what they had wished for.

Once, as a parent, you have learned to let go, you can convey an attitude of confidence and support, backed by calmness and wisdom, even while your children are facing or experiencing failure. No more lectures, no more lessons, no more nagging, no more hidden urgency. Now there is room for your children to discover vital lessons, to share expert opinions, to include you in plotting new ways of conquering their worlds. You and your children can enjoy each other as never before once you abandon the *Make-Sure Parenting* role and put your children in charge.

You will be surprised by the outcome of letting go. Your children will feel challenged by the opportunity to be in charge. They will try to prove to you that they can fulfill their obligations successfully without your help. Unfortunately for your children, their initial attempts to prove their worth may be disappointing. They may fail to get up in the morning without help. They may not be very productive during work time. However, they will soon rise to the challenges of life and begin to grow strong.

Your children will become more motivated and hungry for success once they are free of parental control. Their growth after each failure will provide all the evidence you need that you are on the right track. Your confidence and self-esteem as a parent will grow. You will know that nature is backing you. When challenges come, and your children begin to succeed, they will find the experience exhilarating. They will glow with pride once they have succeeded.

I have asked numerous mothers what has helped them to master the process of letting go. These mothers had been deeply involved in daily Control Poker battles. Their AD/HD children were developmentally at a standstill, their families dysfunctional. By simply relinquishing their *make-sure* roles, most of these mothers have witnessed tremendous growth in their children.

These mothers reported the following factors as having been helpful in their efforts to let go: (1) realizing how their *make-sure* efforts had led to nothing but immaturity and problems; (2) realizing that their children needed help badly; (3) having confidence in a professional who exuded confidence, and gave them permission to let go and try something different; and (4) seeing my simple prediction come true. The prediction was that their children would take pride in their abilities once they felt in charge, and once their success mattered to them more than to their parents. I also predicted that the children would set the highest standards for themselves under these conditions — a sign of their inner parenting ability kicking in and taking over. On the other side of the coin, I predicted that their children would turn off and become difficult once the parents wanted success for their children more than the children wanted it for themselves.

This prediction underscores the importance of parents accepting whatever limitations their children settle for. No more living vicariously through children's accomplishments. Parents must endure living supportively with children who, for significant periods of time, are failing to realize their potential. In due time, this level of acceptance will foster the development of vital abilities in children.

Parents who suffer from severe neurosis will not be able to relinquish control over their children, no matter how hard they try. This is due to the trauma they carry from having been in a position of extreme stress for so long. They may have allowed others to exploit them, because they had grown accustomed to giving way too much. They may have been mistreated and taken for granted by those they have helped the most. Stress has a way of becoming traumatic, and trauma has a way of producing irrational worry.

You can still make this program work even if you suffer from serious parental neurosis. But you will need regular counseling to process your worries about your children. As you relinquish your *make-sure* role, however, you will see your children's inherent strength and their ability to succeed take over. You will begin to enjoy them in a new way. This will ultimately bring your excessive worry to an end.

Intervention 3: Using Family to Teach Social Skills
Respect: The Key to Resolving Social Skills Problems

We all need respect because, when it comes from those who matter to us, it makes us important. It doesn't make us feel important. It truly makes us important. We all have the power to make others important by giving respect and knowing how to demand it. You get respect by giving respect. When you give it, you bring out the best in others. You can help your children develop social skills by dispensing consequences that encourage respect for the family. Your AD/HD child can learn respect for parents, siblings, the belongings of others, school work, and growth.

The root of social skills problems is in not understanding respect, how to give it, and how to command it. In putting their needs ahead of others, the disrespectful convey the message that others are less important than they are. This initiates a cycle in which others return the disrespect, and brings out the worst in those who surround you. I can't begin to count the number of potentially magical friendships that have reached a premature end because of something as petty as one child taking the bigger half of a doughnut. The other person interpreted this as a mark of disrespect, and stopped investing in the friendship.

Obviously, your children need self-discipline to offer true respect. Self-discipline means the ability to make your own personal needs seem less important, so you can gratify the wishes and needs of others. Without self-discipline, the most respect you can offer is lip service: "I wish I could help, but my favorite TV show is on."

The key to initiating friendship is in giving. The key to maintaining friendship is in balancing give and take. This requires a commitment to fairness. You can promote self-discipline by establishing the primary importance of family over individuals, and respect by instilling an ethic of fairness in the family.

Fairness Contract

Several elements can be combined to establish the concept of fairness in the family, formalized in the Family Fairness Contract (**Appendix B**). I include the following three components in the work ethic: (1) every individual managing his own responsibilities; (2) everyone performing an equal share of the communal duties; and (3) everyone avoiding doing harm to others. Begin by introducing those key points to your children. Say something like:

In reference to personal affairs: "Family fairness means you manage your personal affairs. I manage mine. You get up in the morning, get ready for work, earn your day's pay, come home, clean your own room, do your own homework, do your own laundry. I do mine. That's fair. You don't have to come to my office to talk to my boss because I blew my responsibilities, and I don't have to go to your school and talk to your teachers because you blew yours. That's fair."

In reference to communal responsibilities: "In addition, fairness demands that we all share equally in communal duties. Picking up the house, assisting in kitchen duty, and maintaining a pleasant atmosphere in the household, especially during the times the family is working together, and at the dinner table. Each person should also take equal responsibility for any other difficulty that may arise unexpectedly. There are urgent circumstances that complicate things for everyone, and these occur regularly. For example, the washing machine can break and the house can be flooded. This kind of emergency is not Mom or Dad's problem. It's the family's problem."

And in reference to preventing harm: "Finally, fairness demands that each of you avoid harming yourself, or the rest of the family. This includes damage to property, to other family members, to the family atmosphere, to the progress of anyone's education, or to their future, social standing, or health. Considering all the freedom and autonomy we are granting you, it makes sense for you to avoid unnecessary risks. After all, if you are hurt, Mom and Dad have to drop everything to take care of the problem. If you take unnecessary risks, you may become accident prone, and we will end up worrying about you whenever you go out."

The Order of Importance

The *Order of Importance* addresses the priority in which obligations should be met. Communal duties come first, then individual responsibilities, then work or school and self-improvement, and, last, relationships with peers and other forms of self- indulgence. All family members must have enough self-discipline to defer personal needs until last. Family members can use their ability for self-discipline to maximize their manifestations of respect for others.

The Order of Importance allows everyone in the family to discharge their obligations in their own way, and in their own time, as long as they don't indulge in privileges they haven't earned, including time spent with friends, watching TV, or even in self - improvement, while communal duties remain unfulfilled.

You do not have to get your children to agree with the sample Fairness Contract shown in **Appendix B**. It is set up as a guide to the conditions of gaining family privileges. Most older children will welcome the Fairness Contract. By all means have them sign it. Post it, and live by it. However, if your children are oppositional, convince them that the contract is not optional. Family members must, in fact, live under these conditions to gain privi-leges. Of course, you can negotiate and adjust the contract to suit your family's needs, but try to design something as close to this as possible.

The Fairness List

The *Fairness List* is an every day, pragmatic instrument for implementing the Order of Importance and the Fairness Contract. It should be updated regularly, but not obsessively. We create a list whenever we feel that family members have let their responsi-bilities lapse. The standard should be once a week, on the week-end. These are contributions to be made to the family in addition to routine responsibilities, which were layed out in the segment on routine Hotspots. Rather than moan and complain, we write down what hasn't been done. Experts in AD/HD like Russell Barkley have established the importance of devices such as lists to overcome the disability involved in AD/HD. Lists bring the future and the needs of others into the present. Without them, immature and AD/HD individuals are lost.

The Fairness List should include all individual responsibili-ties, including taking care of personal space, school work, and com-munal duties like kitchen work or taking out the garbage. The Fair-ness List should include areas for self-improvement. This legiti-mizes the contribution to the family that comes from positive ac-tivities and self-development.

Feel free to call your family's list a *Complaint List* if your child is in an oppositional-defiant state. Fairness is a positive construct. Oppositional-defiant children want to spoil. Principles of reverse psychology call for utilizing negative constructs with oppositional children, for these pull for a positive response. The Fairness List becomes a Complaint List when things to get done are allowed to go undone for a while. Eventually, you complain that these things should have been done. You write down what needs to be done, and either cut privileges, or set a time when privileges will be cut off if work hasn't been completed.

School and the Fairness List

It is important to decide whether to include homework and school performance on the Fairness List. Technically, failure to complete school work is a misbehavior directed at teachers, not parents and family. This places homework and school performance in the allow zone. It means buffering the natural consequences that school dispenses for failing to complete homework, but only if the buffer is necessary to prevent trauma. However, in some cases the buffer to prevent failure could be a structure at home that helps the child complete the work. One way to provide such a structure is to place homework in the dispense zone, list it on the Fairness List, and make family privileges contingent upon its completion. In other cases, the pressure of placing homework on the Fairness List will only cause family problems. It is generally better to allow and buffer school failure in such cases. Let the willingness to do school work or accept help come from within the child.

We suggest that you try to get away with placing homework in the dispense zone, if you can, and if you think the structure of the Fairness List will help your child succeed. If the child responds to it without much struggle, problem solved. If the child responds adversely, switch it back to the allow zone, where this Hotspot truly belongs.

Follow these general principles when considering the relationship between school work and the Fairness List:

1. Make homework a mandatory part of the Fairness List

for elementary school children. We don't want them to turn out illiterate.

2. Put homework on the Fairness List for older children who are willing to have it there without challenging it.

3. Leave homework off the Fairness List for children who will protest it, and would prefer to forego family privileges rather than complete homework.

If you end up placing homework in the allow zone, and off the Fairness List, take these steps:

Establish respect at home, and support the way your child decides to deal with school life. Have faith that your child will eventually develop the necessary internal drive to succeed in school. Explain to your child that he has simply not developed an appreciation for learning. There is, in fact, such a thing as a late bloomer, and there is adult education for individuals who have missed out on earlier opportunities. Education is a privilege that you develop a taste for after being without it. Failure in school is a healthy thing if accompanied by humor and seen as a learning experience. Contrary to what may be your expectations, failure and the freedom to choose to remain uneducated will eventually be replaced by the desire to learn.

Buffer your child's failure in school by expressing friendship and acceptance, and the conviction that willingness to learn will come with life's challenges. Buffer the failure by letting teachers know that your child is free to fail academically, but must remain respectful. Explain how this is an attempt to prevent your child from being alienated by school. The freedom to fail brings with it the freedom to succeed. With these buffers firmly in place, stop worrying about school. This will induce maximum separation anxiety and *make-sure* functions in your child vis-a-vis school. It will also optimize the friendship between you, which will set up the effectiveness of the next step.

Once your child has experienced the disappointing effects of one or two poor report cards, suggest a philosophy that will allow the love of learning to flourish. Encourage your child to do poorly in classes he dislikes, but take pride in one or two classes that he does like. This will show the child that he has a problem with certain kinds of learning, but not others. This will help your child realize that he can succeed.

The above steps represent expectations for a child who is failing in school. They are calculated to match the child's abilities. If the child doesn't respond in a constructive way after a couple of poor report cards, seek professional help. By then, your child will feel more responsive. I have seen this process produce a dramatic impact on turned-off students numerous times.

Implementing the Fairness List

The implementation of the Fairness List is simple. It is treated exactly like routine Hotspots. You hand out a written list of jobs. Failure to complete them becomes a Hotspot, and a misuse of the privilege of having a household. It impacts the family directly, which puts you in the dispense realm. The misuse of the home calls for the Off Privileges consequence. The reparation is to complete the tasks on the list. This fits the Consequences and Reparations Chart perfectly. This intervention is treated separately because there is a preferred way to make contributions to the family for social skills purposes.

Once you generate your list, you hand it to your child and establish a deadline, the time at which you will quietly turn off all access to the peer world. You casually, and with non-threatening body language, warn your child that he may lose family privileges at that time. You dispense the consequence at deadline-time if jobs haven't been completed. You start by cutting off the electronic peer world, including TV, video games, computer games, telephone and stereo. You are also Off Duty to your child, so no favors, money, or rides, and no friends over.

You can go to your neighborhood electronics store for advice on how to rig your house to cut off access to these Hook Items. It's been my lifelong ambition to produce a device that accomplishes this for five dollars or less. I don't recommend the honor system for most cases. The cutoff is irreversible. It must be emphasized that it will stay in effect until things have been made fair. Otherwise, the child may be tempted to sneak or stuggle to put them back on.

You don't push your child to fulfill the responsibilities on his list. He can simply choose to play games, go outside, exercise or take a nap. You don't want to know when or how the duties are discharged. Remember, your child is in charge. All you know is that soon he will come to you with a completed list, because he will crave access to the peer world he has lost. Just wait and watch children initiate the work on the list. Remember that many vital *make-sure* brain functions involve the process of initiating action. In the absence of parental prodding, your own child will learn to self-start.

Some parents will suffer when their children take too long to clean up their messes and complete their chores. These parents want things done well, but may have to put up with an untidy house for days if the work assigned isn't completed on schedule. The children may have had to function without parental supervision, and the quality of their work may turn out to be substandard. You have to accept short-term consequences like this, however. So important are the long-term development of your AD/HD child and the resolution of oppositional-defiance that you must make these goals the number one priority of your life. The long-term gains will by far outweigh the consequences. Paul Wenning, in his book Winning the Cooperation of Your Child (1995), emphasizes this point. It is well established in the literature.

Once your Off Privileges child comes to you pleading for access to privileges, you use the Shuffle and ask, "Is your list done?" You do not answer the request for privileges. You do not say no. Saying no puts you between the child's need and the outside world. Shuffling means getting out of the middle. If the child claims the list is done, you inspect. You ascertain that the job is complete, or that your child made a reasonable effort. If you are satisfied, you return his access to privileges. If the tasks were not completed satisfactorily, on the other hand, you Shuffle out of the situation and tell the child what remains to be done. You may want to make a note on the written list to that effect. Let the child struggle to develop those healthy *make-sure* functions.

Conclusion

The *Natural-Consequences Program* differs from established approaches in its emphasis on strengthening weak brain functions and fostering maturation. Other methods seek to supplement weak brain functions by providing temporary crutches. I have emphasized the importance of closing the gap between the child's capabilities and the expectations of those around him as a way of bringing about healthy development. Expectations that are too high or too low can lead to developmental arrests.

I have emphasized the importance of addressing ODD and narcissistic tendencies in dealing with AD/HD and other difficult children. I have argued that important needs must be met to help children outgrow fixations at the dependent and oppositional stages of development. These fixations cause the ODD and immature narcissism. I have identified the emotional obstacles that come with the dependent and oppositional stages of development. These can be mastered by offering non-belonging and failure to the oppositional child, and humbling to the dependent, narcissistic child. This forms the basis for the popular intervention that is Time Out.

I have introduced the concept of *Make-Sure Parenting*, the child-rearing method responsible for the failure of most parenting programs tested to date. *Make-Sure Parents* strive to control the uncontrollable, impulsive child, and, in doing so, fall prey to Control Poker tactics. I have introduced the Wheel of Life as a metaphor for how parents are on the go all day, every day. I have pointed out that children use three distinct tactics to jam their parents' Wheel of Life — badgering, dawdling, and personal attacks.

Parents, and particularly mothers, who have been unable to deal successfully with their AD/HD children tend to develop a host of problems, the most prominent being anxiety. They often have extreme difficulty conquering their need to protect their children so they can enable themselves to accept, allow or dispense the necessary experiences of failure and humbling. I have called this set of problems parental neurosis. If the need to protect is strong enough, parents are advised to go for counseling to process their excessive worry while they execute the *Natural-Consequences Program.*

This book has introduced a parenting approach called *Natural-Consequences Parenting,* which borrows heavily from Attachment Theory. It shows how to be playful, but not helpful. This approach allows parents to meet important emotional needs and buffer children from trauma, yet have the child experience sufficient stress from responsibilities to mature and grow strong.

Those of us who are carrying out the program successfully in dealing with AD/HD and other difficult children have learned how to utilize behavioral technology to strengthen adaptive brain functions. We have borrowed the technology of Time Out and learned to extend it to older children and special situations. We have combined the smart consequences of losing misused privileges with reparations that help build a healthy conscience. We have used these basic tenets of behavior modification to anticipate and prepare consequences for routine Hotspots.

We have learned how to build a foundation for confidence by putting kids in charge of themselves, and have learned how to look at failures as learning opportunities, rather than as occasions for shame. Children learn that freedom means the right to run their own lives outside of home in their own way, but it also means increased responsibility at home. I used these explanations to launch the program.

In developing the program, I introduced an intervention called the *Natural-Consequences* Shuffle to escape the oppositional child's Control Poker tactics, with its three steps of join, complain, and walk away. The child jams your Wheel of Life with badgering, dawdling or personal attacks, and keeps you in a state of discomfort until you "lose it" or agree to a payoff. The Shuffle helps you escape these coercive tactics, and prepares you to deliver the consequences you planned.

The last sections of the program entailed special applications of the same method for delivering consequences. One entailed making family interests come first in the child's mind in order to teach self-discipline and respect, the two factors I consider critical to the development of successful social relationships. The second special application sought to end oppositional-defiance. This entailed delivering consequences that resolve narcissism and teach respect.

The final intervention described in this book used the term Hook Items to address the privileges lost by the narcissistically-entitled child. Hook Items drive these children. They are related to the peer world, either the electronic peer world of TV, video games, stereo and telephone, or the flesh-and-blood peer world, consisting of having friends over, rides, money for activities, club memberships, and sports activities.

I realize that we have covered a lot in this book. The purpose of it is to introduce you to concepts, offer you ideas you can use, and serve as a training tool and a reference once you have been trained. The kinds of problems covered in this book are usually severe enough to require professional help during the implementing of the *Natural-Consequences Program*. You should realize that before being exposed to the program the kids described here have been through years of therapies and thousands of dollars in evaluations, and derived only minimal benefits from these considerable efforts. This program offers you a very good chance to truly turn your difficult, AD/HD, or ODD child around. It can be completed in a matter of a few months, although you will require some follow-ups. We expect to be around to increase our understanding of these disorders, and offer you continued help. Thank you for supporting our work.

Appendix A

Quick Reference Guide

The spelling out for children of rights, duties and obligations involving home and family is an important aid to successful parenting. Following are some suggestions on how to do it.

House Rules

1. We are all responsible for ourselves — we dress, feed, groom and clean up after ourselves as much as possible. Older children, twelve and up, help out with younger ones as needed.
2. It's OK to make mistakes — this is how we learn, and grow strong!
3. Be honest — always tell the truth.
4. We respect each other. Respect means to make something important. In our family, everyone's wishes are important and need to be respected.
5. We all have the right to privacy.
6. Be safe at all times.
7. No hitting or hurting with words — be kind at all times.
8. Share it or lose it! — Playing is a privilege. Play well or lose it.
9. Meal times are family time — quiet fun is welcome, wild fun is not.
10. Older kids are the leaders when age differences are three or more years. Leaders need to set a good example for younger kids. Be gentle, let them go first, and show them the right way to behave.

House Lists

Family members agree to distribute work evenly among themselves, and to create a list of duties for each person. The list divides the tasks in order of priority — family jobs first, personal duties second, personal interests third, fun and friends fourth. You can base your House Lists on the following samples.

Grade School Children

Name: _____ Date: _____

Family Duties

- Pick-up duty: Help maintain a picked-up house in all communal areas, including bathrooms, kitchen, basement and yard.
- Kitchen duty: Help with set-up and pick-up duties at mealtimes. This includes food preparation and dish washing.
- Entertainment duty: Help maintain a positive family atmosphere, especially during kitchen and pick-up duty and during family outings.
- Take out garbage.
- Mow lawn.
- Shovel snow.

Individual Duties

- Get up in the morning and be ready on time for the school bus. An alarm clock is strongly recommended.
- Brush teeth.
- Bathe.
- Do homework.
- Clean own room.
- Get ready for bed.

- Prepare clothes and school materials for the next morning.
- Go to bed early enough to get sufficient sleep.

Upper School Children
Name:_____ Date: _____

Family Duties
- Pick-up duty: Help maintain a picked-up house in all communal areas, including bathrooms, kitchen, basement and yard.
- Kitchen duty: Help with set-up and pick-up duties at mealtimes. This includes food preparation and dish washing.
- Entertainment duty: Help maintain a positive family atmosphere, especially during kitchen and pick-up duty and during family outings.
- Take out garbage.
- Mow lawn.
- Shovel snow.

Individual Duties
- Clean room.
- Do own laundry.

House Privileges
- The House provides love, food, clothing, shelter, and protection from outside influences and unreasonable authority. These fundamental privileges are not removable. When in doubt, The House sides with the children.
- The House provides vacations, TV, stereo, computer, telephone, video games, peer world access, private space, cash, and transportation, all earned by completing the work on the House Lists.
- The House supports the privilege of playing with siblings and

friends. The privilege of playing with siblings must be earned by playing well. This means having fun, sharing, and keeping each other from getting hurt, physically or emotionally.

The Order of Importance
- Family obligations come first. These include responsibilities in areas of the house that everyone uses, including living rooms, playrooms, bathrooms, kitchens, and the yard.
- Individual duties are next. For each person, these include maintaining that individual's private space, fulfilling personal responsibilities: cleaning own bedroom, doing homework, doing own laundry, attending to personal hygiene, getting up in the morning, going to sleep at night, and planning and preparing for social activities.
- Personal interests and hobbies are third. These include the children's team memberships, music and art lessons, and other similar activities.
- Lounging, fun and friends come fourth. This includes going to friends' houses, sleep-overs, or having kids over. It also includes the electronic peer world, with TV, stereo, video games, computer, and phone. All of these are House Privileges.

Appendix B

The Family Fairness Contract

I, _____ , agree to the following:

1. That fairness means equal importance of needs, everyone handling equal amounts of communal duties, individual responsibilities, personal development, and prevention of harm. All burdens will be shared equally.

2. I will fulfill my communal responsibilities to family first, then my individual duties at home and work, then self-improvement, and then social life. When there is a legitimate conflict, family comes first, work second, and peers and play third.

3. I will use my freedom wisely, and minimize harm. I will avoid taking risks that would worry my family, and I agree to take reasonable care of my health. If I inadvertently cause anyone harm, including myself, I agree to make fair reparation to the extent of my ability to do so.

4. I will help maintain a good family atmosphere. I will not show disrespect to any family members or guests.

5. If there are deadlines or other time constraints that my family is obligated to meet, I will do my share to keep the family on time, even if it means giving up a fun activity. I will not hold the family hostage by becoming difficult until they meet my personal demands, especially in public or when the family is under the pressure of time.

In exchange:

1.   The other members of my family agree that my social life is extremely important. Therefore, they will support my spending as much time with my friends as I need, once my responsibilities have been met. They will also support safe ways to gain status, like the clothes I wear, or activities that help me fit in.

2.   My family agrees that TV, video games, stereo music, computers, and telephone represent important access to the peer world and are, therefore, very important to me. They agree to grant me access to all of these, once I have made things fair with my family, and fulfilled my school/work obligations.

3.   My family agrees that, as long as I get things done, it is my business how I accomplish them. I am free todo things my own way, as long as I don't cause harm.

4.   My family agrees that once I have met my responsibilities and made things fair, I can run my social and personal life whatever way I think will help me succeed in the eyes of those who matter to me, as long as I don't cause harm to myself or others.

Signed:_____ Date:_____

Following is an example of a Fairness List. Feel free to use it as a template. Customize one list for each child. You must remember to keep a copy, in case your child decides to shred the document. I recommend a computer-generated list, since, in that way, you can create an unlimited number of copies, as well as edit to keep the list up to date. This is a lot more efficient than creating a brand-new list for each family member each time you want work done. You can make lists for the adults also, if you think this will help.

The Fairness List

Name: _____ Date: _____

Individual Duties
- Get up in the morning, be ready for school, and on time for the school bus.
- Make best effort at school.
- Do all homework.
- Report to parents on all long-term assignments.
- Get things ready for the next morning the night before, including clothes and books.
- Maintain a clean room.
- Keep good personal hygiene (brush teeth, bathe).
- Get to bed on time to get enough sleep.
- Do own laundry.

Communal Duties
- Pick-up duty: Help maintain a picked-up house in all communal areas, including bathrooms, kitchen, basement, and outdoors.
- Kitchen duty: Help with set-up and pick-up duties for each meal.
- Entertainment duty: Help maintain harmony, especially during kitchen and pick-up duty, and during family outings.
- Meet family-established deadlines (parent must list specific time for completion of duty).
- Take out garbage.
- Take out recyclables.
- Mow lawn.
- Shovel snow.

Appendix C

Designing Your Own Chart

The chart on the following two pages prepares you to design your own Consequences and Reparations Chart. The top two rows take you through the decision process that you will use to come up with consequences and reparations for the routine Hotspots you anticipate in your household. The top row describes the steps of the allow process for situations that impact primarily on the child's life outside the home, at school and among peers. The second row describes the steps of the dispense process for situations that impact directly on family life. Begin each row with the step in the left column, and work your way to the right, just as in reading left-to-right. The rows below the top two present examples of common, and a few not so common, Hotspots. Review this chart and then use the worksheet that follows to create your own Personal Consequences and Reparations Chart. You will need to clarify these consequences before you begin to implement this program.

Hotspot	Impact	Consequence	Reparation/Compensation
List Hotspot	If the Hotspot is directed at child's life outside of home, then...	the parent allows the consequence to happen, but buffers the consequence if it is too harsh.	No reparation is required, because the Hotspot impacts the child only. Compensation may be required to pay for buffer. List compensation:
	If the Hotspot is directed at the parent and family then...	the parent dispenses the consequence by causing the child to lose a specific item, or by putting the child Off Privileges, or going Off Duty.	After dispensing, child must do: reparation for the infraction; and compensation for the family's wasted time and hardship endured, if applicable.
ROUTINE EXAMPLE Missing school bus.	Child.	Allow with written excuse as buffer. Warn teacher that child will be in charge of getting up at home.	No reparation.
ROUTINE EXAMPLE Leaving mess in kitchen (or entertainment room, or bathroom).	Family.	Dispense: specific loss of room, no kitchen privileges (or TV stereo privileges in room, or bathing privileges), or Off Privileges (if others need that room).	Reparation: clean that room thoroughly. If that's not possible, clean another room. Compensation: not needed.
ROUTINE EXAMPLE Insulting parent.	Parent.	Dispense: Off Duty.	Reparation: Give special honor to that parent in front of others for one day. Compensation for ruined activity: help parent with dinner preparation one night.

ROUTINE EXAMPLE Fighting with brother or sister.	Sibling and Family.	Dispense: Off Privileges.	Reparation: play a special game together as best friends for an afternoon. Compensation: clean up room and provide some quiet time for parent.
ROUTINE EXAMPLE Refusing to do chores.	Family and Parent.	Dispense: Off Privileges.	Reparation: complete list of chores. Compensation: only applicable if others incurred extra work. Make up for it with chores that help those affected.
UNUSUAL EXAMPLE Teenager out past curfew.	Family and Parent.	Dispense: Off Duty, teen locked out of house after curfew until next afternoon. Sleep at friend's house. or Off Privileges.	Reparation: teen must come in early and spend a fun evening with parents in which all get to bed early. Compensation: do some chores for worry time and exhaustion.

Consequences and Reparations Worksheet

The following page introduces a model worksheet you can use to design consequences for routine Hotspots. Make enough copies of your own version to cover a variety of Hotspots. Enter the consequences and reparations you establish for each Hotspot on one row of a summary chart like that displayed in the preceeding pages. This procedure should supply you with a one-sheet reference guide when you're in the trenches.

Keeping Track

Supply the information called for below, and use it with your Consequences and Reparations worksheet as a continuing record of how you've been administering the Natural-Consequences Program. Make enough copies to keep you going.

Hotspot	Zone (Allow/Dispense)	Consequence or Buffer	Reparation/Compensation
1.			
2.			
3.			
4.			
5.			
6.			
7.			
8.			
9.			
10.			

Personal Consequences And Reparations Worksheet

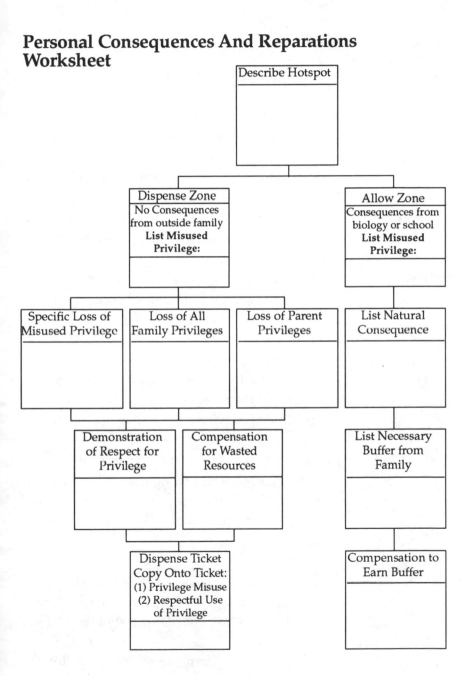

Describe Hotspot

Dispense Zone
No Consequences from outside family
List Misused Privilege:

Allow Zone
Consequences from biology or school
List Misused Privilege:

Specific Loss of Misused Privilege

Loss of All Family Privileges

Loss of Parent Privileges

List Natural Consequence

Demonstration of Respect for Privilege

Compensation for Wasted Resources

List Necessary Buffer from Family

Dispense Ticket
Copy Onto Ticket:
(1) Privilege Misuse
(2) Respectful Use of Privilege

Compensation to Earn Buffer

Glossary

AD/HD   A neurological disorder that impairs a variety of brain functions related to adaptation, including self-regulation, productivity, organization, impulse control, activity, and attention.

adaptive brain   The region of the brain that prevails over impulses, and adjusts to changing environments.

allow   To authorize others outside the family to administer agreed-upon consequences for infractions committed while a child is under their supervision.

attachment   The process by which two individuals bond. Attachment theory seeks to explain much of the irrational behavior of humans.

badgering   Persistent demands and oral attacks directed by a child at parents, designed to interrupt the parents' other activities. Distressing sounds will continue until a desired payoff has been achieved.

black box   A metaphor used by behavior modification theorists to represent internal mental processes thought to occur, but not directly measurable.

buffer   Steps taken by parents to protect their children from consequences likely to debilitate or traumatize them.

cognitive
: Mental operations related to logical thought.

consequences
: The results of behavior.

Control Poker
: The term used to describe mental sparring between parent and child as the parent attempts to enforce his will, and the child employs various devices to avoid compliance. Inevitably, in this contest to determine who has the power, the parent loses his composure and the child prevails.

dawdling
: Acts of dragging, delaying, and stalling when the family needs to prepare for or engage in some joint activity.

dispense
: Consequences administered by parents for infractions that will not involve action by sources outside the family.

emotional intelligence
: A series of mental operations related to adaptation, and popularly held to be associated with success in life.

Hotspots
: Conflict-laden situations that occur routinely in families.

Humble Status
: A state of reduced importance children must

undergo to regain family privileges. Children serve Humble Status to compensate for having made their needs inappropriately more important than those of the family.

intervention   A technique designed to interrupt maladaptive patterns and promote healthy behavior.

make sure   Words used to describe adaptive brain functions in laymen's terms. Make-sure parenting describes a parasitic relationship between children and parents in which the parents perform all the tasks necessary to satisfy their children's needs.

narcissism   An early stage of development during which children are self-centered, self-absorbed, and prone to placing their own needs ahead of the needs of others. Narcissistic individuals tend to suffer from over-inflated egos. They tend to idealize themselves and those around them. Conversely, they tend to devalue and become angry with those who fail to meet their needs.

oppositional-defiance   A developmental stage in which children are negative, blame others for their own infractions, and are driven by the need to spoil things for others. Children in oppositional-defiant states tend to oppose the wishes of others, and defy those who try to force them to do things.

parental neurosis	A state of excessive worry and urge to control that overcomes parents who attempt to perform *make-sure* brain functions for their resistant children.
privileges	Benefits offered by families to create opportunities for its members, and thus advance their development.
reparations	Demonstrations of respect for privileges that have been misused. Reparative acts are positive contributions to family. The result should be to undo the effects of harm done to others, and compensate family for significant inconveniences caused by infractions.
separation anxiety	States of worry and discomfort resulting from the absence of parents. Separation anxiety tends to occur when children realize they are facing consequences without parental protection. Low levels of separation anxiety foster the development of new mental abilities in children.
Shuffle	A maneuver designed to escape Hotspots. It involves a joining statement, a complaint, and walking away. The maneuver is designed to offer the child encouragement and time to think, and the parent time to determine the appropriate consequence, and prepare to deliver it. The Shuffle interrupts the tit for tat that may escalate out of control in Control Poker

Time Out   A popular behavioral intervention proven ef-
                    fective with younger children, especially ages
                    four to eight. Time Out temporarily removes
                    the child from contact with the family, and can
                    be effective in interrupting tantrums and other
                    difficult behavior, and altering the young child's
                    mood without causing harm.

Wheel of Life   A metaphor for the obligations we all face as
                    parents. It is an exhausting list of responsibili-
                    ties, especially when approached from the per-
                    spective of the Make-Sure Parent with an AD/
                    HD child.

Technical Sources

Abikoff, H. & Klein, R. (1987). *Cognitive training in treatment of hyperactivity in children.* Archives of General Psychiatry, Vol. 43(3), 296-297

Abikoff, H. & Klein, R. G. (1992). *Attention-deficit hyperactivity and conduct disorder: co-occurrence and implication for treatment.* Journal of Consulting and Clinical Psychology, Vol. 60, 881-892.

Abikoff, H. (1987). *An evaluation of cognitive behavior therapy for hyperactive children.* In B.B. Lahey & A. Kazdin (Eds.), Advances in Clinical Child Psychology. (Vol. 10, pp.171-216). New York: Plenum Press.

Abikoff, H. (1991). *Cognitive training in ADHD children: less to it than meets the eye.* Journal of Learning Disabilities, Vol. 24, 205-209.

Abikoff, H., Klein, R., Klass, E., & Ganeles, D. (1987). *Methylphenidate in the treatment of conduct disordered children.* In H. Abikoff (Chair), Diagnosis and Treatment Issues in Children with Disruptive Disorders. Symposium conducted at the Annual Meeting of the American Academy of Child and Adolescent Psychiatry, Washington, DC.

Ainsworth, M. D., Blehar, Walters, & Wall (1978). Patterns of Attachment: A Psychological Study of the Strange Situation Patterns of Attachment: A Psychological Study of the Strange Situation. New York: Halsted Press.

Albin, J. B., Lee, B., Dumas, J., Slater, J., & Witmer, J. (1985). *Parent training with Canadian families.* Canada's Mental Health, Vol. 1985, 20-24.

Alexander, S. (1973). Learning How to Study Behavior: An Interdisciplinary Approach. South Hadley, MA: [s. n.].

Allen, J. P., Hauser, S. T., Bell, K. L. & O'Connor, T. G., (1994). Longitudinal assessment of autonomy and relatedness in adolescent-family interactions as predictors of adolescent ego development and self-esteem. Child Development, Vol. 65(1), 179-194.

Amatea, E. S., & Sherrard, P. A. (1991). *When students cannot or will not change their behavior: Using brief strategic intervention in the school.* Journal of Counseling and Development, Vol. 69(4), 341-344.

Anastopoulos, A. D., Guevremont, D. C., Shelton, T. L., & DuPaul, G. J. (1992). *Parenting stress among families of children with attention deficit hyperactivity disorder.* Journal of Abnormal Child Psychology, Vol. 20(5), 503-520.

Baden, A. D. & Howe, G. W. (1992). *Mothers' attributions and expectancies regarding their conduct-disordered children.* Journal of Abnormal Child Psychology, Vol. 20(5), 467-485.

Baker, A. K., Barthelemy, , K. J., & Kurdek, L. A. (1993). The relation between fifth and sixth grader's peer-classroom social status and their perceptions of family and neighborhood factors. Journal of Applied Developmental Psychology, Vol. 14(4), 547-556.

Balthazor, M. J., Wagner, R. K., & Pelham, W. E. (1991). The specificity of the effects of stimulant medication on classroom learning-related measures of cognitive processing for attention deficit disorder children. Journal of Abnormal Child Psychology, Vol. 19, 35-52.

Bank, L., Patterson, G. R., & Reid, J. B. (1987). *Delinquency prevention through training parents in family management.* The Behavior Analyst, Vol. 10(1), 75-82.

Barkley, R. A. (1987). Defiant Children. A Clinician's Manual For Parent Training. New York: Guilford.

Barkley, R. A. (1989). *Hyperactive girls and boys: stimulant drug effects on mother-child interactions.* Journal of Child Psychology and Psychiatry and Allied Disciplines, Vol. 30(3), 379-390.

Barkley, R. A. (1990). Attention-Deficit Hyperactivity Disorder: A Handbook For Diagnosis And Treatment. New York: Guilford.

Barkley, R. A., Anastopoulos, A. D., Guevremont, D. C., & Fletcher, K. E. (1992). Adolescents with attention deficit hyperactivity disorder: mother-adolescent interactions, family beliefs and conflicts, and maternal psychopathology. Journal of Abnormal Child Psychology, Vol. 20(3), 263-288.

Barkley, R. A., Fischer, M., Edelbrock, C. & Smallish, L. (1991). The adolescent outcome of hyperactive children diagnosed by research criteria: iii. Mother-child interactions, family conflicts and maternal psychopathology. Journal of Child Psychology & Psychiatry & Allied Disciplines, Vol. 32(2), 233-255.

Barkley, R. A., Fischer, M., Edelbrock, C. S., & Smallish, L. (1990). The adolescent outcome of hyperactive children diagnosed by research criteria: an 8-year prospective follow-up study. Journal of the American Academy of Child and Adolescent Psychiatry, Vol. 29(4), 546-557.

Barkley, R. A., Guevremont, D. C., Anastopoulos, A. D., & Fletcher, K. E. (1992). A comparison of three family therapy programs for treating family conflicts in adolescents with attention-deficit hyperactivity disorder. Journal of Consulting and Clinical Psychology, Vol. 60, 450-462.

Basch, C. (1988). Between freud and lacan, the post-freudians: ernst kris and the case of "mental anorexia." Revista de Psicoanalisis, Vol. 45(3), 553-559.

Baum, C. G. & Forehand, R. (1981). Long term follow-up assessment of parent training by use of multiple outcome measures. Behavior Therapy, Vol. 12, 643-652.

Bernal, M., Klinnert, M., & Schultz, L. (1980). Outcome evaluation of behavioral parent training and client-centered parent counseling for children with conduct problems. Journal of Applied Behavioral Analysis, Vol. 13(4), 677-691.

Biederman, J., Munir, K., & Knee, D. (1987). *Conduct and oppositional disorder in clinically referred children with attention deficit disorder: A controlled family study.* Journal of the American Academy of Child and Adolescent Psychiatry, Vol. 26, 777-784.

Boszormenyi-Nagy, I. & Krasner, B. (1986). Between Give and Take:

A Clinical Guide to Contextual Therapy. New York: Brunner Mazel.

Bowlby, J. (1969). Attachment and Loss. New York: Basic Books.

Braswell, L., Koehler, C., & Kendall, P. (1985). Attributions and outcomes in psychotherapy. Special issue: the emergence of research at the interface of social, clinical, and developmental psychology. Journal of School and Clinical Psychology, Vol. 3(4), 458-465.

Burland, J. R. (1986). *One of the familyóa behavioral approach.* Maladjustment and Therapeutic Education, Vol. 4(2), 74-79.

Bustamante, E. (1992). Play and Pride: For Spirited Children and Their Families. Amherst, MA: Play and Pride.

Campbell, S. & Ewing, L. (1990). *Follow-up of hard-to-manage preschoolers: adjustment at age 9 and predictors of continuing symptoms.* Journal of Child Psychology and Psychiatry and Allied Sciences, Vol. 31(6), 871-889.

Campbell, S. B. (1985). *Hyperactivity in preschoolers: correlates and prognostic implications.* Clinical Psychology Review, Vol. 5(5), 405-428.

Carlson, C., Pelham, W., & Milich, R. (1992). Single and combined effects of methylphenidate and behavior therapy on the classroom performance of children with attention deficit — hyperactivity disorder. Journal of Abnormal Child Psychology, Vol. 20(2), 213-232.

Cassidy, J. (1988). Child-mother attachment and the self in six-year-olds. Child Development, Vol. 59(1), 121-134.

Christensen, A., Johnson, S., Phillips, S., & Glasgow, R. (1980). *Cost effectiveness in behavioral family therapy.* Behavior Therapy, Vol. 11(2), 208-226.

Conners, C. K., Kramer, R., Rothschild, G. H., Schwartz, L., & Stone, A. (1971). *Treatment of young delinquent boys with diphenylhydantoin sodium and methylphenidate.* Archives of General Psychiatry, Vol. 24, 156-160.

Dangel, R. F., Deschner, J. P., & Rasp, R. R. (1989). Anger control training for adolescents in residential treatment. Special Issue: Empirical research in behavioral social work. Behavior Modification, Vol. 13(4), 447-458.

Douglas, V. I., Barr, R. G., Amin, K., O'Neill, M.E., & Britton, B. G. (1988). *Dosage effects and individual responsivity to methylphenidate in attention deficit disorder.* Journal of Child Psychology and Psychiatry, Vol. 29, 453-475.

Dumas, J. E. (1984a). Interactional correlates of treatment outcome in behavioral parent training. Journal of Consulting and Clinical Psychology, 52(6), 946-954.

Dumas, J. E. (1984b). Child, adult-interactional, and socioeconomic setting events as predictors of parent training outcome. Education and Treatment of Children, Vol. 7(4), 351-364.

Dumas, J. E. & Wahler, R. G. (1983). Predictors of treatment outcome in parent training: mother insularity and socioeconomic disadvantage. <u>Behavioral Assessment,</u> Vol. 5, 301-313.

Eisenberg, L. Lachman, R., Molling, P. A., Mizelle, J. d., & Conners, C. K. (1963). *A psychopharmacological experiment in a training school of delinquent boys.* <u>American Journal of Orthopsychiatry,</u> Vol. 33, 431-447.

Evans, R., Gaultieri, C., & Amara, I. (1986). *Methylphenidate and memory: dissociated effects in hyperactive children.* <u>Psychopharmacology,</u> Vol. 90(2), 211-216.

Ferber, H., Keeley, S., & Shemberg, K. (1974). Training parents in behavior modification: outcome of and problems encountered in a program after patterson's work. <u>Behavior Therapy,</u> Vol. 5(3), 415-419.

Fischer, M. (1990). *Parenting stress and the child with attention deficit hyperactivity disorder.* <u>Journal of Clinical Child Psychology,</u> Vol. 19(4), 337-346.

Forehand, R., Middlebrook, J., Rogers, T., & Steefe, M. (1983). *Dropping out of parent training.* <u>Behavior Research Therapy,</u> Vol. 21(6), 663-688.

Frankel, F. & Simmons, J. Q (1992). *Parent behavioral training: why and when some parents drop out.* <u>Journal of Clinical Child Psychology,</u> Vol. 21(4), 322-330.

Gard, G. & Berry, K. (1986). *Oppositional children: taming tyrants.* <u>Journal of Clinical Child Psychology,</u> Vol. 15(2), 148-158.

Gittelman, R., Klein, D. F., & Feingold, I. (1983). *Children with reading disorders: ii. Effects of methylphenidate in combination with reading remediation.* Journal of Child Psychology and Psychiatry, Vol. 24, 193-212.

Gottfried, A,E., Fleming, J.S. & Gottfried, A.W. (1994). *Role of parental motivational practices in children's academic intrinsic motivation and achievement.* Journal of Educational Psychology, Vol. 86(1), 104-113. [PA, Vol. 81:31446]

Greene, B. A., Royer, J. M., & Anzalone, S. (1990). *A new technique for measuring listening and reading literacy in developing countries.* International Review of Education, Vol. 36, 57-68.

Griest, D. L. & Wells, K. C. (1983). *Behavioral family therapy with conduct disorders in children.* Behavior Therapy, 14, 37-53.

Haenlein, M. & Caul, W. (1987). *Attention deficit with hyperactivity: a specific hypothesis of reward dysfunction.* Journal of the American Academy of Child and Adolescent Psychiatry, Vol. 26(3), 356-362.

Haley, J. (1973). *Strategic therapy when the child is presented as the problem.* Journal of the American Academy of Child Psychiatry, Vol. 12(4), 641-659.

Haley, J. (1984). Ordeal therapy. San Francisco: Jossey-Bass.

Harter, S. (1978). Effectance motivation reconsidered: toward a developmental model. Human Development, Vol. 21(1), 34-64.

HButchn, B. L., Parrish, J. M., McClung, T. J., & Kerwin, M. E. (1992).

Using guided compliance versus Time Out to promote child compliance: A preliminary comparative analysis in an analogue context. Research in Developmental Disabilities, Vol. 13(2), 157-170.

Heslin, R., & Patterson, M. (1982). Nonverbal Behavior and Social Psychology Nonverbal Behavior and Social Psychology. New York: Plenum Press.

Hinshaw, S. P. (1992). Academic underachievement, attention deficits, and aggressions: co-occurrence and implications for intervention. Journal of Consulting and Clinical Psychology, Vol. 60, 893-903.

Hollingshead, A. B., & Redlich, F. C. (1958)). Social class and mental illness. New York: Wiley.

Horn, W. F., & Ialongo, N. (1988). Multimodal treatment of attention-deficit hyperactivity disorder in children. In H. E. Fitzgerald, A. H. Lester, & M. W. Yogman (Eds.), Theory and Research in Behavioral Pediatrics, (Vol. 4, pp. 175-219). New York: Plenum.

Horn, W., Ialongo, N., Pascoe, J., Greenberg, G., et al. (1991). Additive effects of psychostimulants, parent training, and self-control therapy with adhd children. Journal of the American Academy of Child and Adolescent Psychiatry, Vol. 30(2), 233-240.

Horn, W., O'Donnell, J., & Vitulano, L. (1983). Long-term follow-up studies of learning disabled persons. Journal of Learning Disabilities, Vol. 16(9), 57-68.

Jacob, T., Krahn, G. & Leonard, K. (1991). Parent-child interactions *in families with alcoholic fathers.* Journal of Consulting and Clinical Psychology, Vol. 59(1), 176-181.

Johnson, K. R., & Layng, T. V. J (1992). *Breaking the structuralist barrier: literacy and numeracy with fluency.* American Psychologist, Vol. 47, 1475-1490.

Kazdin, A. E. (1987). Treatment of Antisocial Behavior in Children and Adolescents. Homewood, IL: Dorsey Press.

Kazdin, A., Bass, D., Siegel, T., & Christopher, T. (1989). *Cognitive-behavioral therapy and relationship therapy in the treatment of children referred for anti-social behavior.* Journal of Consulting and Clinical Psychology, Vol. 57(4), 522-535.

Kendall, P., Reber, M., McLeer, S., Epps, J., et al. (1990). *Cognitive-behavioral treatment of conduct-disordered children.* Cognitive Therapy and Research, Vol. 14(3), 279-297.

Klein R., & Last, C. (1989). Anxiety Disorders in Children. Newbury Park, CA: Sage Publications.

Landau, S. & Moore, L. (1991). Social skills deficits in children with attention deficit — hyperactivity disorder. School Psychology Review, Vol. 20(2), 235-251.

Lewis, M., Feiring, C., McGuffog, C., & Jaskir, J. (1984). *Predicting psychopathology in six-year-olds form early social relations.* Child Development, Vol. 55(1), 123-136.

Lochman, J., Burch, P., & Curry, J. (1984). *Treatment and generaliza-*

tion effects of cognitive-behavioral and goal-setting interventions with aggressive boys. Journal of Consulting and Clinical Psychology, Vol. 52(5), 915-916.

Lochman, J., Wayland, K., & White, K. (1993). *Social goals: relationship to adolescent adjustment and to social problem solving*. Journal of Abnormal Child Psychology, Vol. 21(2), 135-151.

Long, N., Ricket, V. I., & Aschraft, E. W., (1993). Bibliotherapy as an adjunct to stimulant medication in the treatment of attention-deficit hyperactivity disorder. Journal of Pediatric Health Care, Vol. 7, 82-88.

Mahler, M. S., Pine, F., & Bergman, A., (1975). The Psychological Birth of the Infant: Symbiosis and Individuation. New York: Basic Books.

Main, M., Kaplan, N., & Cassidy, J. (1985). *Security in infancy, childhood, and adulthood: a move to the level of representation*. Monographs of the Society for Research in Child Development, Vol. 50(1-2), 66-104.

McMahon, R. & Wells, K. (1989). *Conduct disorders*. In E. Mash & R. Barkley (Eds.), Treatment of Childhood Disorders. (pp. 73-132). New York: Guilford Press.

McMahon, R. J., Forehand, R., & Giest, D. L. (1981). Effects of knowledge of social learning principles on enhancing treatment outcome and generalization in a parent training program. Journal of Consulting and Clinical Psychology, Vol. 49(4), 526-532.

Meharg, S. S. & Lipsker, L. E. (1992) *Parent training using videotape self-modeling.* Child and Family Behavior Therapy, Vol. 13(4), 1-27.

Meihenbaum, D. (1977). Cognitive Behavior Modification: An Integrative Approach. New York: Plenum Press.

Meihenbaum, D. (1990). *Paying homage: providing challenges.* Psychological Inquiry, Vol. 1(1), 96-100.

Minuchin, S. (1974). Families and Family Therapy. Cambridge, MA: Harvard University Press.

Moffitt, T. E. (1990). Juvenile delinquency and attention deficit disorder: boy's developmental trajectories from age 3 to age 15. Child Development, Vol. 61, 893-910.

Murphy, D., Pelham, W., & Lang, A. (1992). Aggression in boys with attention deficit — hyperactivity disorder: methylphenidate effects on naturalistically observed aggression, response to provocation, and social information processing. Journal of Abnormal Child Psychology, Vol. 20(5), 451-466.

Nathan, W. A. (1992). Integrated multimodal therapy of children with attention-deficit hyperactivity disorder. Bulletin of the Menninger Clinic, Vol. 56(3), 283-312.

O'Dell, S. L., Mahoney, N. D., Horton, W. G., & Turner, P. E. (1979). *Media-assisted parent training: alternative models.* Behavior Therapy, Vol. 10, 103-110.

Olson, D. H., McCubbin, H. I., Barnes, H., Larsen, A., Muxem, M.,

& Wilson, M. (1989). <u>Families: What Makes Them Work</u> (Second Edition). Los Angeles, Sage.

Olson, D. H., McCubbin, H. I., Barnes, H., Larsen, A., Muxem, M., & Wilson, M. (1992). <u>Family Inventories.</u> St. Paul, MN: Family Social Science

Patterson, G. & Narrett, C. (1990). The development of a reliable and valid treatment program for aggressive young children. Special issue: unvalidated, fringe, and fraudulent treatment of mental disorders. <u>International Journal of Mental Health</u>, Vol. 19(3), 19-26.

Patterson, G. R., & Narrett, C. M. (1990). The development of a reliable and valid treatment program for aggressive young children. <u>International Journal of Mental Health</u>, Vol. 19(3), 19-26.

Pelham, W. E. (1986). The effects of psychostimulant drugs on learning and academic achievement in children with attention-deficit disorders and learning disabilities. In J. K. Torgeson & B. Y. L. Wong (Eds.), <u>Psychological And Educational Perspectives On Learning Disabilities,</u> (pp. 259-296). San Diego, CA: Academic Press.

Pelham, W. E. & Hinshaw, S. P. (1992). *Behavioral intervention for attention-deficit hyperactivity disorder.* In S. M. Turner, K. S. Calhoun, & H. E. Adams (Eds.), <u>Handbook of clinical behavior therapy,</u> (2nd ed., pp. 259-283). New York: Wiley.

Pennington, B. & Ozonoff, S. (1991). *A neuroscientific perspective on continuity and discontunuity in developmental psychopathology.* In D.

Cicchetti & S. Toth (Eds.), Rochester Symposium on Developmental Psychopathology, (Vol. 3 pp. 117-159). Rochester, NY: University of Rochester Press.

Pollard, S., Ward, E., & Barkley, R. (1983). *The effects if parent training and ritalin on the parent-child interactions of hyperactive boys.* Child and Family Behavior Therapy, Vol. 5(4), 51-69.

Rapport, M., et al. (1985). Methylphenidate in hyperactive children: differential effects on dose in academic, learning, and social behavior. Journal of Abnormal Child Development, Vol. 13(2), 227-243.

Reeves, J. C., Werry, J. S., Elkind, G. S., & Sametkin, A. (1987). *Attention deficit, conduct, oppositional and anxiety disorders in children. II. Clinical characteristics.* Journal of the American Academy of Child and Adolescent Psychiatry, Vol. 26, 144-155.

Rey, J. M., Bashir, M. R., Schwartz, M., Richards, I. N., Plapp, J. M., & Stewart, G. W. (1988). *Oppositional disorder: Fact or fiction?* Journal of the American Academy of Child and Adolescent Psychiatry, Vol. 27, 157-162.

Ross, J., Mercer, C., & Hendrickson, J. M. (1985). *The multidisciplinary team: Reaching beyond traditional assessment.* International Journal of Partial Hospitalization, Vol. 3(2), 117-129.

Royer, J. M. , & Sinatra, G. M. (1994). *A cognitive theoretical approach to reading diagnostics.* Educational Psychology Review, Vol. 6(2), 81-113.

Royer, J. M. & Carlo, M. S. (1991). Assessing the language acquisition progress of limited English proficient students: Problems and a new alternative. Applied Measurement in Education, Vol. 4, 85-114.

Rutter, M. Tizzard, J., Yule, W., Graham, P., & Whitmore, K. (1976). *Research report: Isle of White studies*. Psychological Medicine, Vol. 6, 313-332.

Sattler, J. (1974). Assessment of Children's Intelligence. Philadelphia: Saunders.

Schachar, R., & Wachsmuth, R. (1990). *Hyperactivity and parental psychopathology*. Journal of Child Psychology and Psychiatry, Vol. 31, 381-392.

Schreier, H. A. (1990). *A multimodality approach to the treatment of children and families*. New Directions for Mental Health Services, Vol. 46, 75-80.

Scott, M. J. & Stradling, S. G. (1987). *Evaluation of a group program for parents of problem children*. Behavioral Psychotherapy, Vol. 15(3), 224-239.

Sherwood, V. R. (1990). The first stage of treatment with the conduct disordered adolescent: overcoming narcissistic resistance. Psychotherapy, Vol. 27(3), 380-387.

Singh, N., Deitz, D. E., Epstein, M. H., & Singh, J. (1991). Social behavior of students who are seriously emotionally disturbed: A quantitative analysis of intervention studies. Behavior Modification, Vol. 15(1), 74-94.

Speltz, M., Greenberg, M., & Deklyen, M. (1990). Attachment in preschoolers with disruptive behavior: a comparison of clinic-referred and nonproblem children. Development and Psychopathology, Vol. 2(1), 31-46.

Stein, D. B., & Smith, E. D. (1990). The "rest program:" a new treatment system for the oppositional defiant adolescent. Adolescence, Vol. 25(100), 891-904.

Sternberg, R. (1985). Beyond IQ: A Triarchic Theory of Human Intelligence. New York: Cambridge University Press.

Stice, E., Manuel & Chasen, L. (1993). Relation of parental control and to adolescents externalizing symptomatology and substance abuse: a longitudinal evaluation of curvilinear effects. Journal of Abnormal Child Psychology, Vol. 21(6), 609-629.

Talbot, F., Pepin, M., & Loranger, M. (1992). *Computerized cognitive training with learning disabled students: a pilot study.* Psychological Reports, Vol. 71(3, Pt 2), 1347-1356.

Vostanis, P., Nicholls, J., & Harrington, R. (1994). *Maternal expressed emotion in conduct and emotional disorders of childhood.* Journal of Child Psychology & Psychiatry & Allied Disciplines, Vol. 35(2), 365-376.

Wahler, R. (1980). *The insular mother: her problems in parent-child treatment.* Journal of Applied Behavior Analysis, Vol. 13(2), 207-219.

Walker, H. M., Retana, G. F., & Gersten, R. (1988). *Replication of the CLASS program in Costa Rica: Implementation procedures and program outcomes.* Behavior Modification, Vol. 12(1), 133-154.

Walker, L. & Taylor, J. (1991). *Family interactions and the development of moral reasoning.* Child Development, Vol. 62(2), 264-283.

Webster-Stratton, C, Kolpacof, M. & Hollinsworth, T. (1988). Self-administered videotape therapy for families with conduct problem children: Comparison with two cost-effective treatments and a control group. Journal of Counseling and Clinical Psychology, Vol. 56, 558-566.

Webster-Stratton, C. (1985a). Predictors of treatment outcome in parent training for conduct disordered children. Behavior Therapy, Vol. 6, 223-243.

Webster-Stratton, C. (1990). *Long-term follow-up with young conduct problem children: from preschool to grade school.* Journal of Clinical Child Psychology, Vol. 19(2), 144-149.

Webster-Stratton, C. (1991). *Annotation: Strategies for helping families with conduct disordered children.* Journal of Psychology and Psychiatry, Vol. 32(7), 1047-1062.

Webster-Stratton, C. (1992). *Individually administered videotape parent training: "Who benefits?"* Cognitive Therapy and Research, Vol. 16(1), 31-35.

Webster-Stratton, C., Hollinsworth, T., & Kolpacoff, M. (1989). The long-term effectiveness and clinical significance of three cost-effective training programs for families with conduct-problem children. Journal of Consulting and Clinical Psychology, Vol. (4), 550-553.

Weiss, G. & Hechtman, L. T. (1986). Hyperactive Children Grow Up: Empirical Findings and Theoretical Considerations. New York: Guilford Press.

Werry, J. S., Reeves, J. C., & Elkind, G. S. (1987). Attention deficit, conduct, oppositional and anxiety disorders in children: I. a review of research on differentiating characteristics. Journal of the American Academy of Child and Adolescent Psychiatry, Vol. 26, 133-143.

Wetchler, J. L. (1986). *Family therapy of school-focused problems: a macrosystematic perspective.* Contemporary Family Therapy: an International Journal, Vol. 8(3), 224-240.

Whalen, C. & Henker, B. (1991). *Therapies for hyperactive children: comparisons, combinations, and compromises.* Journal of Consulting and Clinical Psychology, Vol. 59(1), 126-137.

Whalen, C., Henker, B., & Buhrmester, D. (1989). *Does stimulant medication improve the peer status of hyperactive children.* Journal of Consulting and Clinical Psychology, Vol. 57(4), 545-549.

Winnicott, D. W. (1971). Playing and Reality. New York: Basic Books.

Woltersdorf, M. A. (1992). *Videotape self-modeling in the treatment of attention-deficit hyperactivity disorder.* Child and Family Behavior Therapy, Vol. 14(2), 53-73.

To order additional copies of PARENTING THE
AD/HD CHILD: A NEW APPROACH, call:

1-800-354-1789

Outside of the U.S. call: 413-737-9630

Whitcomb Publishing
32 Hampden Street
Springfield, MA 01103